The Heart Writing Handbook

A JOURNEY INTO THE MAGIC OF HEART-LED
WRITING AND STORYTELLING

The Heart Writing Handbook

ROSE MASCARO
Founder of HeartWriting®

HEARTWRITING

First published by The Kind Press in 2025
Copyright © Rose Mascaro 2025

All rights reserved. No part of this book may be reproduced by any mechanical, photographic or electronic process, including AI-generated reproductions, or in the form of a phonographic recording, nor may it be stored in a retrieval system, transmitted, or otherwise copied for public or private use other than for 'fair use' as brief quotations embodied in articles and reviews without prior written permission from the publisher.

Cover design and illustration by Zalia Lackey
Author photo credit: Ingrid Sjodahl Photography
Typeset in 12/17 pt Minion 3 by Post Pre-press Group

 A catalogue record for this book is available from the National Library of Australia

ISBN: 9781763800953 (paperback)

The intent of the author is only to offer information of a general nature to support your education and wellbeing. The author and publisher make no representations or warranties of any kind, express or implied, about the accuracy, completeness or suitability of the content for any purpose. In the event you use any of the information in this book for yourself, neither the publisher nor the author accepts any liability for any loss, damage or disruption arising from reliance on the information contained in this book. This includes but is not limited to direct, indirect, incidental, special or consequential damages. By engaging with this material, readers acknowledge personal responsibility for their own choices and actions.

The Kind Press acknowledges all Aboriginal and Torres Strait Islander Traditional Custodians of Country and recognises their continuing connection to land, sea, culture and community. We pay our respects to Elders past and present.

*It all starts by placing a hand on your heart
and listening to the author within.*

*This book is dedicated to every HeartWriter
who has touched my heart with their words.*

Rose Mascaro is an Australian writer, editor and teacher who is passionate about teaching others how to connect with their most authentic, heart-led words. She's the former editor of *Teen Breathe* magazine, Australia's leading mindfulness magazine for teens, and holds a master's degree in creative writing from UTS, Sydney.

In a previous life, Rose spent over a decade as a secondary English teacher in her hometown of Perth. Hearing the calls of her creative heart, she quit her job, travelled the world, studied yoga and meditation, and moved to Sydney to complete her MA in creative writing. She became a writer and editor specialising in fiction, travel, spirituality and lifestyle. In 2020 Rose launched *HeartWriting®* Australia where she teaches powerful, authentic writing from the heart using a combination of literature, meditation, spirituality, heart theory, and creative psychology. Her sellout writing workshops and retreats are a perfect blend of spiritual connection and writing technique. Rose has authored two books, is published in magazines and anthologies internationally, and has co-authored a range of Australian titles.

heartwriting.com.au
@heartwriting.com.au

Contents

Part One: Shedding// let go of fear and ego
Chapter One: Writer wakes up — 3
Chapter Two: Fear of the writer — 23
Chapter Three: Ego of the writer — 35
Chapter Four: Emotion of the writer — 45

Part Two: Surrender// listen to your heart
Chapter Five: The heart of the writer — 61
Chapter Six: Spirit of the story — 79
Chapter Seven: Silence, meditation, movement — 99
Chapter Eight: Buddha nature in the writer — 123

Part Three: Success// master your craft
Chapter Nine: Crafting the story — 135
Chapter Ten: Authentic voice — 149
Chapter Eleven: Mastery — 159
Chapter Twelve: Community — 175
Chapter Thirteen: Devotion to completion — 187
Chapter Fourteen: Full circle — 201

Recommended Reading — 215
Endnotes — 217

At HeartWriting, *we honour the deep, unbroken storytelling traditions of the First Nations peoples of the Lands on which we work and share stories today – the original Keepers of Wisdom, Language and Lore. We are deeply committed to fostering an inclusive, diverse and equitable space where all writers, regardless of background, identity, or experience, feel welcome, safe and empowered to share their voices and stories with open hearts.*

I grew up – and became an aspiring writer – on the Lands of the Whadjuk people of the Noongar Nation in Fremantle, Western Australia. I acknowledge the Whadjuk people as the Traditional Custodians of this Land, and I pay my respects to their Elders past and present. This place shaped me: its coastal winds and ancient earth carrying stories long before I ever tried to write my own.

Today, I craft my narratives on the shores of Avoca Beach on the Central Coast of New South Wales. I acknowledge the Darkinjung people, and their neighbouring Nations and Clan Groups, as the Traditional Custodians of this Land, and I pay my respects to their Elders past and present. Their presence and stories remain woven into the forests, mountains and sands I walk on each day.

PART ONE
Shedding

Let go of fear and ego

CHAPTER ONE

Writer wakes up

somewhere on the edge of the world

It had been my intention to write a book on my year of travels, but I found my way onto every dance floor instead. 'Why write, when you can live!' I screamed to myself every time I found myself on a bar table, or knocking back a shot of tequila, or scaling yet another volcano. I had stories banked up like chapters of a book – and yet, I hadn't written many of them. By the time my laptop was stolen I felt secretly relieved. Partying, adventuring and escaping seemed safer than *actually* conquering my dreams.

Before the trip I'd walked away from the two biggest chapters of my life – my career as a high school teacher, and my marriage – leaving trails of heartbreak and chalk dust behind me in a single breath. And now, all alone, battling a persistent flu while perched at altitude in the freezing cold Peruvian Andes, I was forced to stop. I took a breath, and asked myself the big question: *If I'm supposed to be a writer, then why aren't I writing?*

The answer, of course, was in my heart, its pulse quickening like the beat of a shamanic drum: *It's because I'm too scared to write. To fail as a writer.*

And yet – I'd just climbed every volcano and every mountain in every country I'd conquered in Central and South

America. I'd navigated dangerous border crossings, lost my way in winding cities, and had guns pointed at my face. But if I put pen to paper, and I sucked, then how utterly *ashamed* would I feel?

This sweet little town in the Sacred Valley of Peru forced me to sit down and face my fears. I'm *so* glad I stopped here, for more than this reason. Pisac is a stunning treasure for those on the sojourn to Machu Picchu: a town spilling with history, cultural treasures, precious stones and incense, all wrapped up with ubiquitous smiles and fluffy white alpacas strutting the streets. Despite my tears, I couldn't say I was mad about being here. The place was breathing the life back into me. I wiped my eyes and watched Peruvian women strolling with weaved baskets propped on their heads, exuding an inner peace that stirred the attention of the whole valley.

There was one other good reason why I was so devastated. My new travel friend, Jack, whom I'd hiked Machu Picchu with over July, had just left Peru to return to Australia. We'd spent the last few weeks joined together at the hip – sharing hostel rooms, carrying each other's bags, mending each other's sickness and injuries, accompanying each other to dinners, having those big conversations about life. He wanted to get out of carpentry, I never wanted to go back to teaching. Every conversation was *a sign*. Suddenly I felt very attached to this Jack, and on our last night together – in the pretty white volcanic city of Arequipa – we giggled our way down a cobblestone alleyway towards the melody of pan flutes, ordered another round of Pisco Sours, and shared the rest of our ravenous dreams.

Yet we both knew all of this would soon be over. Jack was booked on a flight back to Sydney the next day. I couldn't imagine the next six months *not* travelling with him.

So here I was a few days later, now all alone in the mountains of Peru, in the midst of a sacred pause. A pause I much needed. Tears rolled like a ritual down my cheeks. *Finally,* I thought, and wiped my tears with the sleeve of my flannel shirt, picked up my notebook, and wrote it all down. *Ah, there she is*, I thought to myself. *It's been a while.* My heart cracked right open then and there, and she fell all over my lap in a puddle of grief and love.

Surrender, silence, remembrance

Of course it's not easy to deny your heart's calling as a writer when you've darted from distraction to distraction like a *Race Across the World* contestant. My heart's compass arrow had been spinning like a top trying to redirect my course away from the partying, the people, the destinations, the drama, the tequila. But now the spinning slowed. Silence and tears softened my fall, and my heart showed me who I really was: *A writer. A philosopher. A big heart.*

I just needed to remember that I once had been a brave, bold and talented little writer with no qualms in telling the world. At seven years old I sat in my cubby house curating my very first book collection: the first of many. I wrote out all the final copies in pen after several pencilled drafts. I designed a book cover and planned my backyard launch. I laid out my books on the patio table, my rough pencil designs and bold headings displayed to the world. 'My world' consisted of six people: my family and a couple of neighbours.

20c a book. They paid. *I am an author.*

Perhaps, just like me, you're a born writer who has words breathing life from your bones: a conscious, smart, heart-led creative who thinks deeply about the crossroads between art, spirit, and science. You've read Gabor Maté back-to-back. You've booked to do your yoga teacher training *and* a solo trip to Nepal next winter. You go to therapy, you're well in tune with your past traumas, and you'll still have a wine and a boogie afterwards, because you have balance.

This person – *you* – desperately wants to write the story of your adventures, tragedies and successes. Even better – you want to pen a *beautifully* crafted book that could change the world. Problem is, it's hard knowing where to start as an aspiring writer when the world keeps telling you *you're doomed to fail.*

Why I really stopped writing (aka long before my travels)

Back when I was a kid charging 20 cents a pop for a book, I was blissfully unaware that there was stigma in the world about being a writer. I shaped magical worlds into words, and penned those words onto paper, and to me, very important people do that. I loved the feeling, and my family loved my gifts, too.

Until, of course, I hit high school – and writing wasn't on the career list. Journalism, at best. Thinly veiled words rose like secondhand cigarette smoke from adults and career counsellors. 'Writing? What kind of job will that get you? Be a bit more practical. You'd make a good lawyer.'

We've all been told that artistic talent cannot be relied upon, *because it's not necessary to create art*. Food is necessary. Houses are necessary. Apparently only the luckiest people in the world can exist as self-sufficient creatives. I get the stigma, I really do – and I'm not angry about it, because there's good reason for it. In the 20th century, the World Wars and the Great Depression took centre stage. For our parents or grandparents, there was no time or money left to indulge in the arts. No wonder we've been brainwashed to believe that the arts are reserved for the rich or the lucky few.

In the end, I believed the well-told story, but only halfway.

Ok, so I *did* follow my dreams to complete a degree in creative writing at university – *how very cool and bohemian of me!* – but in a surge of uncertainty at the finish line, I dropped the journalism honours and instead went into English teaching. The *safe* career. So there I was at 22, *not* a writer, but a teacher.

We become what we believe, and therefore I created my

very own reality by not trying at all. And this became a habit, a trend, a self-fulfilling prophecy. I'd been brainwashed into a state of fear: a self-protection mechanism from inevitable failure.

But the truth is, it wasn't just the Great Depression that killed the writer. Colonialism and capitalism had killed the arts long ago. Writers and books aren't necessary in our conveyor-belt world. And I'm OK with that if people need to eat, live, survive. But suddenly, multi-million-dollar mortgages are necessary? $10,000 watches and handbags are necessary? Celebrity football is necessary?

Why is art not necessary? Creation not necessary? Something has gone massively awry.

And so artists – like us – are constantly sabotaging ourselves before we even start. Because if we don't try, we don't have to feel the shame of failure. We don't have to feel rejected by peers or family. Take me – I had all the privileges in the world, and still I felt the sharp fangs of people's biting views. But there was no real reason why I should have failed. There were tonnes of opportunities for budding writers and creatives at the time. Still are.

If only I'd tried. *But I ran in the other direction.*

I wonder how different things would have been if I'd been offered more emotional and societal support as a young artist. I might have embedded a much more confident belief system; I might have conquered my dreams much earlier. Was it any wonder that, on the trip of a lifetime, with money to support me for an entire year, and all the time and inspiration to write, I was *still* not writing?

But anyway, I am *not* here to wallow in regrets. After all, there's a journey to embark upon, and without the journey, there would be no story to write, and no lesson to learn.

Back to Peru (and back to pen and paper)

There I was, crying myself back to life in the middle of nowhere, perched at the edge of the world in a small country town about a million miles from home. I was sick. I was alone. I was tired. I'd been on the road – mostly solo – for six months, and I had six months of the trip left. My laptop had recently been stolen and I'd taken it as my biggest sign yet.

But I pulled out my notebook, anyway – because I had to. Because my heart told me to. Nestled under a tree that I likened to my own Bodhi, I wrote and wrote and wrote. I wrote the madness and friendship and love and memories and tears out of me. A feeling of euphoria rushed through my veins. *This feeling of writing is everything.*

After my writing session, my inner hell seemed far more like heaven. I looked around and noticed the majestic mountains that surrounded each face of the town. I took out my camera and snapped a photo of the view – and then of my tear-splotched face – to seal the memory of this moment.

Opening, listening, writing from the heart

My crumpled heart was now ripped wide open and I wanted to remember this feeling of pain and joy and humble awakening, forever. It felt good to *feel so much*, and to write, and to heal from expressing these precious words on the page.

'You need to face your fears. You need to make a life out of what you love,' my heart told me.

I still have the photo of my tear-stained face on that day in the mountains, at my rock bottom, on the cusp of my biggest spiritual and creative awakening. I realised that my heart had been calling me for a very long time. I just wasn't ready yet to listen, until this moment – where it felt like God was shouting a message at me, from my very own heart, that *I could be a writer if I wanted to.*

Later that day the crux of my future travel novel came to me while travelling on a bus to the next town. On this bus a little Peruvian girl kept popping her head up from her seat to look at me. I was entranced by her. I soon fell asleep and dreamed an intensely real dream about waking up to find the bus parked and empty, except for the little girl stranded and crying in her seat. It was my quest to find out why she'd been abandoned. But yes, this was all a dream. I woke some time later, dazed – and saw that we were all still bobbing along on the bus, and the little girl was still in her seat, playing with her doll, occasionally looking back and smiling at me, *la gringa*. She was just as entranced by me as I was by her.

But the *dream*: I had to write it down, in that very moment. It felt bigger than me. The words drifted magically to my fingertips and my journal pages exploded like a cauldron of voices, faces, words, textures, smells, the song of story.

I still have those pages. And one day I rewrote those pages to create my first novel.

It's all in the details

I saw the little girl one last time – when the bus journey really ended. Spooked that I would get left behind on the bus, I stuffed all my things into my bag, shuffled down the aisle, and burst into dusty sunlight. A line of people, including the girl and her parents, stood beside the bus to retrieve their luggage. While waiting, I took in all her fine details – the pink beanie, the flushed pink cheeks, the shy smile. *Remember this moment, and remember her,* the voice of my heart told me, and I knew that I needed to secure this image forever, as she would become very important to me and my future book.

Since that magical day in Peru I've become passionate about writing the words without fear. I've also become passionate about listening to my heart, because *now I know* it always leads me in exactly the right direction. After a lifetime that didn't quite feel right – yet looked so good on paper – it made perfect sense that I needed to drop the act and start listening to my heart.

And funny enough, listening to my heart required me to drop all the other distractions that were just muffling the clarity of my calling.

My heart is my true North compass

My little beating heart, filled with 40,000 neurons and an inbuilt 'life GPS' – had led me to embark on this awe-inspiring and wildly dangerous trip – a journey that encouraged me to face danger and get creative on a daily basis.

My heart had taken me to the quietest and most sacred town in South America, smack in the middle of my travels. It sat me down hard and said: *Just listen – shut the hell up and listen. All the gifts and abundance are inside you.* And once I was open to listen, the story and the words came.

But I would be remiss if I didn't acknowledge my immense privilege in being able to pay for this trip – one that allowed me to access cultural, geographical, and economic diversity, as well as my own private awakening.

I now recognise how opportunity, not just hardship, magic, or luck, shaped my path. In my younger days I romanticised my journey – as many do. But with time, experience, and sensitivity, I see more clearly how privilege opens doors that remain closed to others. This awareness humbles me and fuels my passion for helping creatives pursue their dreams – without privilege being the prerequisite to their golden ticket.

But guess what? The most valuable ticket that everyone holds in their hands is their own authentic story.

Gathering stories and confidence (to write)

The best thing about my year-long solo travels was that everything was wildly imperfect – which gave me stories to write! I lost things, I gained things. I witnessed things, I failed to witness things – I was just a naïve big kid living a very wild life. I realised that I'd not had much life experience at all. This trip *gave me stories to write, and the courage to do something with them.*

And so I returned home, and my visions became very clear. I kept listening to my heart. I moved across Australia to study my master's degree in creative writing. I became a writer and editor: first in magazines, then in books.

FUN FACT

Most people say <u>masters</u> with no apostrophe, when in fact, it is a master's degree. Just like 'editor's letter' needs an apostrophe. That's just one of the many little things I learned, which took me to my next exciting chapter as an editor in the publishing industry.

But, you know, once you take a few giant leaps in life, the leaps start to feel less scary. My heart spoke once more. *Take another leap.*

And soon *HeartWriting* was born.

Here we are. I write every day and I work with writers every day: teaching my craft, editing others' crafts, and writing books. But mostly my job is to challenge people to defy their fears and dance with their creative destiny.

So many people are desperate to write, but are too tangled up in their heads and *'what ifs'* with barely any belief in themselves to take the next step. I hope you are reading this with that creative little glimmer in your eye that says, *yes – I believe it is possible, and I'm opening my heart and mind to 'what's next'.*

The Heart Writing Handbook will take you on a thrilling exploration of what it takes to become a successful and sustainable writer through learning the magic, science and spirituality of the heart: your greatest tool when it comes to writing. In fact, we'll travel through all three stages of *The HeartWriting® Method:*

1. **Shedding (let go of fear and ego)**
2. **Surrender (listen to your heart)**
3. **Success (master your craft)**

From shedding fears, dodging the ego, learning how to open the heart, slowing down from a high-speed life, and savouring the craft of words, you'll be taken on a meaningful journey that will transform you into a fearless writer ready to take on your dreams.

Don't forget that your art *is worth fighting for*

I want you to know that *your words are a balm to the world*, and eventually, you must listen to your heart's callings to release those words to those who need them. By the end of this book, you'll be a fully-fledged *HeartWriter*: someone courageous enough to *open their heart* and *create lasting change from the page*. Because your brave words can inspire a world that is in dire need of them.

Over fourteen glorious chapters we will explore the expansive truths and faulty myths I have experienced as a writer. I'll explain my major setbacks and rapid fast-forwards and everything in between. We'll discuss the heart-strangling topic of *fear* and how to overcome it with spirituality, meditation and embodiment. We'll explore the science and history of storytelling, and why writing is *never* going anywhere, despite our fears that writing is dead.

Most of all, you'll learn about the role of the heart in getting back to the page.

Luckily, I listened to my heart and pushed through, because I've now discovered the other side of the rainbow, and yes, the grass is greener here, with *The HeartWriting® Method* on my side – as a professional writer and editor. Yes, now I am a writer. An author. And yes, my words have become a balm to the world in a variety of ways I never could have known if I'd never had the courage to write them. And now it's time for you to write yours, too.

Circle back to Jack

Let's rewind again to that day in the little town in the Sacred Valley. I'm crying over my departed friend, Jack. So what happened to him? Did we reunite? What did I do next? You're invested in the story already, aren't you?

Isn't storytelling powerful?

Of course, in true narrative style, I'm not spoiling the climax yet. I'll tell the rest of the Peru story at the end of this book. But in the meantime, I want you to read this book in whatever order you like. I'm not into rules for rules' sake. As a creative writer and reader, *following your intuition* is your gold. If your heart says so, read the end first and then flip backwards. You can read random chapters in non-linear order, even though the book is in some kind of order. You can question, and compare, and come back to the start, and read it all again. That's how I read, and live my life, anyway. *I have to make my own mistakes*, and I rarely play by the rules. Even this book wasn't written by the rules. The creative life is like a complex jigsaw puzzle with a few missing pieces. The more I fill the gaps with my own unique zest, the more I am rewarded.

> **The creative life is like a complex jigsaw puzzle with a few missing pieces. The more I fill the gaps with my own unique zest, the more I am rewarded.**

DOING THE INNER WORK TO SHAPE YOUR VISION

Answer these journal questions after resting in a long, luxurious meditation. You can find my guided creativity meditations on the *HeartWriting* podcast.

1. What does creativity mean to me?

2. What are some things I'd like to explore in my writing?

3. What makes me feel uncreative or unworthy of creativity in my life? Are these things actually true? Explain.

4. What are my greatest blocks, excuses and distractions that keep me from writing?

5. Who do I look up to creatively and aspire to be, and why?

6. Am I already like this person in some ways? *Is it possible I can fully embody the qualities I admire in them?*

7. Is there anything still holding me back from stepping on to my path? Are there some damaging myths out there about being a writer – that don't serve me? Answer this one on a separate piece of paper.

8. Then, burn your answer in a sacred burning ceremony. Say goodbye!

Lastly, write down the opposite statement of the last question. This will become your *HeartWriting mission statement* that allows you to accomplish that obstacle and step on the path. Post it on your bathroom mirror or desk. Savour it daily. Let it become you.

THE HEARTWRITING® METHOD

How to connect with your highest creative writing potential, and write with ease, authenticity, precision, confidence, and joy.

Meditation and movement

When you meditate, move mindfully, and release thoughts, you can shift stuck energy and clear the clutter from the top layer of your consciousness. This will help you get closely attuned with the authenticity of your voice and the callings of your heart. From there, creative magic can happen – revealing worlds and ideas you've never dreamed of.

The heart and the brain

Lower frequency creative brainwaves like Theta and Alpha are where the magic of the creative process occurs. By meditating frequently and connecting with our hearts we can access these states more often. Children function primarily in the Theta and Alpha brainwaves: a dreamlike state where one can get easily immersed in other worlds. As we get older, our brainwaves speed up and we find it harder to access our imagination, so it's important to lower the frequencies daily.

Spirituality, philosophy, psychology

Your highest creative potential resides in your subconscious and your spiritual heart. Once you connect deeply with your inner spirit, your creativity will soar effortlessly. In the *HeartWriting* curriculum, we dive into ancient Indian and Buddhist philosophy, and the art psychology of Freud, Lacan and Carl Jung, who all studied the subconscious impact of creative pursuits and how they reveal the inner psyche/ spirit.

Read, learn, and write lots

The fastest way to become a confident, strong writer is to learn from the best writers – from the modern and ancient world. Study the techniques that accomplished writers use. Don't get too comfortable with your favourite reads; extend yourself past your comfort zone. Read and write from a mix of cultures, genders, perspectives and eras. And then write, and write.

Creative community

It's important to connect deeply with other creatives – to share writing, give feedback, and discuss the writing process. This helps you grow as a writer. When you write in isolation, you can't gain new perspective on your work – not to mention how enjoyable it is to read other writers' beautiful words.

CHAPTER TWO

Fear of the writer

I'm absolutely terrified to write. I'm terrified you'll analyse every word, laugh with all your friends, and shoot my reputation to smithereens. And there, shit – I've used a pun. A cliché. I'm going to writers' hell. I may as well quit while I'm ahead. Oh, bugger. There I go again.

I'm four years old. Kindergarten. A party.

A long table is piled with jars and cakes and spilling with sandwiches and fruits of the rainbow. Music is playing. Kids are dancing. In a whirlpool of bobbing hands and toothy smiles, I have no idea what is going on – but I'm mesmerised. This has got to be the most EXCITING DAY OF MY LIFE. Suddenly there's a hush and the whole pile of kids and adults crowd around a cake. A cake! And they are singing *Happy Birthday!* Oh – of course! I spot the candles: shimmery flames poking out of melty delicious colourful icing, and I totter all the way around the perimeter of the huge rectangular table until I reach the glorious cake. 'Happy Birthday Dear Rosie – Happy Birthday to you!' I smile, round my lips, and push out a roaring puff. All the candles hiss. *Success.*

And then all the kids start bawling. No – *howling*. I stare in confusion. And then I see the girl whom I've practically climbed over to get to the candles: she's crying the hardest. Oh no ... I've blown out *another girl's* birthday candles? *Happy Birthday Dear ...* But I'm sure they said *Rosie*! My mother appears with hands on hips, brows forming a deep V. It is the first time I remember seeing her looking so stern. *Like, really unhappy.* I reach around her legs for comfort but she won't even look at me. I know I have really, really mucked up.

This feeling has never left me since. I have felt a lifetime of, 'you are going to muck up *anyyy* second now'. And that's basically how it all starts for creatives who are embarking on a lifetime of making art: because there's no direct standards for creativity. We are always potentially blowing out the wrong cake candles when we follow our hearts *with our art*.

But I don't believe our heart can ever lead us astray. I just believe that past traumas can really bugger up our confidence.

New classroom. Same stuff up.

Fast forward thirty years and fresh off my year-long travels, riddled with dreadlocks and high-octane travel stories, I sat in my creative writing master's degree – *finally, doing the thing, you go girl!* – discussing texts with mature age students who all looked and sounded very different to me. I noticed there was a type, an academia, an eyebrow, *an aesthetic*, to writers. Writers who were not like me.

I was at the wrong party altogether. *Damn.* This felt like a horrible case of déjà vu.

The truth is, I don't look like a writer. I don't sound like a writer. I don't dress like a writer. I don't behave like a writer. I don't enjoy genre fiction conventions and I despise writers' forums.* *What the hell am I doing here, trying to complete a master's degree, trying to write a book? Seriously?* That hot-faced feeling of clutching around my mum's legs haunted me, reminding me of what a muck-up I am. *You are not meant to be here. You're not like these people. You're far too loud. Crass. Weird. Hippie. You'll never make it like a [insert writer stereotype].*

But one day I realised that there is no prerequisite to becoming a writer. There is no pressed uniform and no way of thinking that would make me a better writer, other than being exactly *me*. Perhaps the very fact that I so defied the stereotype gave me a leg up in the industry, a fresh perspective, and *a story*.

Once I overcame my identity complex, then came the imposter syndrome. *Are you even a good enough writer, you fraud?* – the evil little voice would snipe at me no matter what I scrawled. Suffice to say, my first semester in my master's degree was brutal. There was a lot of money at stake for me to potentially discover that I simply sucked.

But something shifted – and exceptionally fast. It could have been the therapy sessions I wailed myself through. But it

---

* And I *really* hate the idea of a book launch. The thought of releasing an *actual book* to the world and having to show up at a stuffy venue to read out my work to a group of lukewarm strangers always gave me the icks. But look at me now, baby! – I just had to do things my own way.

doesn't matter how I shifted the problem, because I'd shifted the problem.

I realised that I had been in my own way with all my own excuses the whole time. I didn't need to be a clone of my classmates. I discovered my unique style, which my lecturers loved. It's OK to have fear – just go for it anyway. And my favourite lesson of all: I don't have to be perfect all the time, because practise and mastery cures everything. *(And editing. God bless editing skills).*

Writing Myth #157: Writing is always fun.
(Writing is *not* always fun. And that's OK.)

For some reason we think that writing is magic, limited to the gifted few, and that no training is required. *Maybe a few YouTube lessons is enough.* And because of this we feel ashamed when we don't get anywhere, and terrified of failure. We sabotage ourselves before we've even learned the basics. For me, I ran across the edges of the world to escape from my equal amounts of longing *and shame* for a career that felt so far from reach.

But writing is a conscious craft that is learned like any other skill. The only way to learn to become the writer I'd always known I was destined to become ... was to *open my heart and do the work*. And that meant taking risks, facing fears, and learning it's OK, in fact it's necessary, to fail. Once I had accepted that, the words came easier. I wasn't tethered to perfection. I kept writing.

Life isn't always fun. And writing isn't always fun. All of it: the highs and lows, the successes and failures – this is the exquisite learning journey. *HeartWriting* is all about listening to the callings of your creative heart, and acting on them, despite pain and hardship and doubt. Embracing the chaos and writing through the imperfection. Learning to listen to other hearts. Learning to *learn*. Expressing with unashamed authenticity, rather than perfection and ego.

The great unknowns in art

But there are so many unknowns and uncertainties in producing art. You're making things that don't necessarily run by a tried and tested formula. In fact, the more genius work you are producing, the less likely you are going to be abiding by society's so-called rules. Producing original, creative works means stepping outside of the norms of society. It means taking risks. And we have so many hang-ups about doing something that may not result in success – well, it's no wonder we block ourselves so often from finishing that project. We want to know the success rate before we put it out to the world. *Will people like my thoughts and words? Is this the right dress for the right party? Am I blowing the wrong candles out again?*

Take French artist Claude Monet: when he first revealed his Impressionist paintings, they were dismissed as childish. Now his works are considered pure genius. And this is not a unique story. In fact, most successful artists, writers and musicians did not start out as wildly popular.

What's the story that stands out for you? Are you afraid of failure? Afraid of being poor? Unsuccessful? Afraid of what people might think? Or are you even secretly afraid of success, and how people might judge you, target you, or envy you for your genius?

Gotta start somewhere

Looking back on all my journals, and God forbid, my Facebook posts from 2008, it's very clear that I had a lot of work to do before I could eloquently put any kind of pen to page, let alone be published. I may have known a lot about writing, I may have been a decent writer – but I was still an amateur *and immature* writer, with little wisdom, life experience or perspective to be found in my rambling, attention-seeking, poorly-executed posts.

It's OK though – I'm not shaming myself. And neither should you. It's so important that we look back on these former writings with compassion and acceptance. It's also important that we don't judge other writers on their journeys too. Because writing is a particularly hard craft, and a long road at that. You must simply keep writing. Sharing. Editing. Rewriting. Each year, the writer gets better. Being a prolific writer comes before the profound writer.

For me, it was more than just writing. I needed experiences and I needed stuff to write about. I needed my world view wedged wide open and a hearty boxing match of heartbreak thrown in. When I look back I see a sheltered girl with nothing much to think or say. Writing is a philosophical endeavour, and I didn't have the slightest clue about the meaning of life.

And then, at 30 and 31, I traversed dozens of countries solo and became humbled by the vastness of the world. I hiked the Colombian jungle for five days with ten strangers and two new friends – no reception, no housing, no showers – to arrive at the emerald green platform which overlooked the ancient site of *Ciudad Perdida*: The Lost City of Colombia. Suddenly I had things to write about: the mountains craning in around us; green, crisp. The grubby sunken beds we slept in under the stars. The Argentinian sniper we met who handed us a joint. Where did he get it from? Who knows. We each took a drag as we watched clouds hovering precariously around the edges of treetops:

> *I sighed into the sight in front of us. 'I think I like this a little too much,' I said quietly, handing the joint back. We all stared into the everlasting landscape. I pulled out my notebook and wrote it all down before I could possibly forget this feeling. I didn't want to go back. I didn't want to switch my phone back on when we returned to reception. I took my shoes off and nestled bare toes into the earth of this sacred site. Another life on the other end of the world, shared with people that make my heart stop in time and make my breath catch against the dusty wind ... my feet bare, a ring slipping, a feeling higher than any drug.*

Writing practice and mastery starts with *life*

For me, there was no other option than to get out of my comfort zone and live a very big, loud and scary life – *before* I became a writer. Fear shapes us, and simultaneously holds us back – both as writers, and as people. By getting brave with my life I started to be more brave with my writing.

My honest belief is that you can become a successful and deeply fulfilled creative if you tune in to your heart rather than the fear. I also believe that it's not just about blind belief. It takes a lot of work to become a writer. That's kind of comforting, because it's not just luck – anything can be achieved with hard work. This is called mastery, and according to writer Malcolm Gladwell, it takes ten thousand hours to master anything. So let's put in the hours, and the hearts.

Dare yourself to feel the fear

I know what it's like to *Feel the Fear and Do it Anyway,* just like the book by Susan Jeffers. I eventually faced my fear and started working on my craft. I went to more classes. I workshopped and listened eagerly to critique, treating it as a learning tool rather than a personal attack. With each fear I faced, the more confidence I built towards conquering the next step on my journey.

It doesn't matter what I do with my writing – I know I just need to *keep writing*. I need to keep believing in myself. The more words I write, the more doors keep opening up for me.

Just like the law of attraction, it's all about my beliefs changing first. Sometimes we just need to do the thing, so that we have evidence of the magic that we are creating.

Samantha Jayne Brunskill, Australian business strategist, says that the key to overcoming fears and leaning into greatness is about trusting your inner calling. 'I listen to spirit and act straight away – within five seconds,' she says. 'I learned this rule from Mel Robbins. I then keep my commitments and follow the plan: *not* my feelings or fears.'

Work creates progress, which creates results, which creates evidence, which creates *belief*. And when you tap into your highest powers and faith, the universe cannot ignore you. That's why it's so important to listen to, honour and love your *own* heart first. Because it knows best.

JOURNAL QUESTIONS FOR FACING FEAR

- What are you longing to create?

- Are you afraid your work might not be liked and accepted?

- Are you holding back from completing your project due to other people's self-serving fears and opinions?

- Or are you secretly afraid that success might change your relationships – and your life?

CHAPTER THREE

Ego of the writer

Problem is, you have finally overcome your fear era, only to realise you have entered your ego era. You're now addicted to being 'seen' and 'acknowledged' – all the damn time. You need everyone from your partner to your grandmother to your barista to read your writing – just so that you can get some praise: that smarmy hit of confidence to keep going.

Hello. I'm Rose Mascaro, and I am a praise addict. I want my *writing to be seen*. I want my words to be *recognised*. I don't want to write *for no reason* – what *on earth* is the point in that?

But there is a problem with being a praise addict when you are a writer. This is a vocation that requires long stints of silence. In those extended times of deep writing, like while writing this book – when nobody sees my work for months, or years – I waver in motivation and confidence.

Of course I do. I'm lonely while writing. Lonely as hell! And I know the stats. I know it's so hard to get seen by publishers. So why would I keep doing something that makes me feel so ... horribly ... *unseen?*

From fear to excitement

A few years ago, things were finally going just great. My master's degree was a carnival of moving past my fears – towards excitement and literature and community and all the creative madness I'd so desired. Most of all, it gave me the audience I so needed for my writing. Peers. Lecturers. New creative friends.

It was the sensation of being *seen through my words* that kept me feeling exhilarated. I finished my postgrad on the ultimate high with a HD and a great reference from my head professor. Straight after, my partner and I cruised into the clouds for a two-week diving trip to Indonesia – and just like that, on the plane, it hit me. *I'm still not a writer.*

'That's it. Nobody is ever going to read my work,' I wailed. 'I have no job. No real purpose with this.'

But within hours of landing I forgot about my woes, and it turned out to be one of the best holidays of my life, filled with coral-shimmering waters and cocktail-filled beach parties.

On the flight home, reality set in. The air hostess handed out the customs arrival slips. I searched for a pen and scanned the questions. The 'occupation' question stared at me, and I stared back at it.

What is your usual occupation?   _____

I sighed, pen in hand. 'When *will* I be a writer?' I whined.

My partner smiled at me – a miniature, knowing smile.

He's very familiar with my penchant for drama. 'You decide when. You decide *now*. Come on. Write it down here.'

What is your usual occupation? *Writer*

I looked at my lettering. I smiled. I took a photo of it. He hugged me. *I'm a writer,* I thought to myself.

The second we touched down, I received a voicemail from an Australian magazine publisher for a job interview. I jumped in the shower and scrubbed myself clean. I smoothed down my salt-encrusted curls (more like dreadlocks), threw on my best blazer, and went in – that very day – without a wink of sleep from the red eye flight. Totally unprepared. But I had announced to the universe that I was a writer – and yes, I was offered a job that very day.

<u>Now</u> *I'm a real writer.*

I was given my first writing assignment and it was so exciting. I would come home pointing at my drafts, eager for it to be propped up on a newsstand in colour. This was actually happening.

From excitement to reality

But don't get too excited. See, the publishing industry is slow, quiet, and deeply introverted compared to the quick wins and loud high-fives I'd experienced in my teaching career. I'd entered an entirely different culture of approval, and it felt strange. Why wasn't everyone patting me on the back all the time? And when was my damn article going to be published – so that somebody could praise me?

The reality is that a magazine takes months to make, and more months to put on the market. By the time I wrote one article, which would then make the rounds getting checked by four editors and three designers, I would then have to wait three to six months before that magazine would be up for sale and anyone would see my work.

In between that time I was not allowed to share any words of that article with anyone, or I'd be in breach of my contract. I often sat at my desk thinking, 'this is too slow for me. What's the point of all this?' What I really meant was, 'I'm not getting enough validation to make this feel worth it for me.'

Just a dopamine addict

It's all perfectly understandable, really. We are, after all, human beings – navigating life with brains governed by a delicate balance of chemicals. Cortisol, dopamine, oxytocin to name a few. For a writer like me who craves regular dopamine surges, sometimes the act of writing can feel like driving down a long, endless highway. 'What's the point?' I'd hear myself say over and over again, tossing yet another draft in the bin.

I've got a funny feeling that you relate. But let's go easy on ourselves, because it's not our fault: our brains are not much different to our hunter-gatherer ancestors. We're driven by the pursuit of short-term rewards – dopamine being the main prize. The problem with dopamine is this: just like a drug, we find ourselves needing more and more to feel even a hint of what we once did. Unfortunately, the further away the goal, the less immediate the dopamine reward, which makes writing a particularly hard career for any human.

It's wise to be wary of the dopamine rush. The more immediate pleasure you get from an action, the less likely this will result in your long-term goals or your highest potential for happiness. Instead, play this line on repeat in your mind: *Slow and steady wins the race.* Every time I remind myself of this well-worn adage from Aesop's fables, something softens in me and I'm reminded of the bigger picture of why I'm here.

> **I might be a praise addict, but the long and often impatient road to get here was worth it.**

Slow and steady wins the race.

It's more important to find the virtues in small, consistent habits – steady practices that may not offer immediate rewards but build up over time to create lasting success. This compound effect is where small victories accumulate into something greater. This is why I mentioned in Chapter Two that *writing is not always fun,* but always worth it.

I might be a praise addict, but the long and often impatient road to get here was worth it. Without the discipline that working for a publisher provided, and learning how to achieve long-term goals of the magazine industry, I wouldn't have experienced the shimmery joy of seeing my words in print – way more exciting than those shimmery candles I blew out by mistake when I was four.

Old-school hard work *works*

Every writer must learn the rules first in order to uplevel their words. Sorry if you don't want to hear this, and sorry if you think you have nothing more to learn about writing: but, *you do*. Everyone does, even if you're incredible, accomplished, an absolute natural.

There's *always* more to learn. And that's a great thing.

A.C. Grayling, British philosopher, maintains that humans find the most meaning in life through their challenges and hard times.[1] Think about it: the Industrial Revolution totally changed the world overnight: machines suddenly took the place of human jobs, freeing up time for more fulfilling pursuits. But instead of happiness, records noted a spike in depression. Why? Because hard work is at the heart of humanity. Without it, human growth ceases. And today, similar problems emerge with the rise of artificial intelligence. Sure, things are getting easier, but making things easy disrupts our natural relationship between hard work and joy.

It was so important for me to get over myself and *get on with the work* in order to access my deepest rewards in my writing – far deeper than the short-term thrill of a quick compliment from a rushed social media post or blog.

When writing feels like a lonely grind, remember this: it's

not that you're not cut out for it. It's just your mind craving its next fix. It's your history, your biology, and your personality. But if you stick with small, consistent habits, you'll find your way back to a place where the work feels not just doable, but satisfying, shimmery, and *sustainable*. Like you could do this forever. When we understand this with the same sense of '*wow*' we feel about getting 200 likes on a post, we can start to build better 'slow and steady' habits that support our deeper goals, instead of constantly chasing the next fleeting thrill. And with a little patience, you'll finish that big project – and find insurmountable joy in the process. Goodbye, dopamine, and hello, *Love*.

CHAPTER FOUR
Emotion of the writer

It's 2014 and I'm an emotional wreck. I've just returned from a music gig at my favourite bar. The guitars and vodka are still rattling inside my brain and if I'm completely honest with myself, I really shouldn't have driven home. The slowness of my reflexes – combined with furtive glances for police cars – really wasn't worth the risk. Switching off the ignition in front of my home, I lean back against the leather seats and turn on one last tune on my car stereo before I head into the house. The song is one of those screamy-sad tearjerkers that reminds me of every ruined love. The tears roll down my cheeks as I think about *the guy* who'd arrived at the gig with *another girl*. I pick up my phone and type out all the words that represent the bigness of the feelings that engulf me. I'm suffocating in them.

> *Did you woo her, the way you wooed me?*
> *Did you see all the same things in the gentle sea?*
> *Because there's patterns in my eyes*
> *That only you could realise*
> *And I'm left thinking, but where will we be.*
> *Will you come back to me*

Or will we dissolve
Into the great unknown
And always think of that one star
Of a sacred super moon?

Ugh. I was so addicted to love back then. I would often trick myself into thinking I was such a great writer just because I expressed my words quickly, feverishly, in a trance of emotion. But let's all be very bloody honest: these were definitely not my best words. I just seemed to write *more* when I was emotional.

The emotions are your greatest gift as a writer. They are also your cruellest enemy, because they trick you to lean on them to act on your craft. You become addicted to writing in an emotional state, and this isn't sustainable. Don't be like me in 2014. And definitely don't be like Kurt Cobain, addicted to drama and drugs in order to write great songs. Forget the stereotype of the depressed, emotional, lovesick creative. If you want to last the distance as a writer, and if you want to defy the 'suicidal creative' stereotype, then it's time to ditch your emotions, sweetheart. And I don't just mean 'toughen up.'

I used to write about heartbreak.
Now I have a lot more to say.

Sure, it's true that life experience and emotional depth can enrich our writing, but relying solely on volatile emotions is just plain old addiction. This dependency can often lead to the very writing blocks you're desperate to shake off for good. It's a dangerous cycle.

Ava Irani, meditation expert and creator of Functional Spirituality™, speaks a lot about the emotions in her classes. 'Our generation has been taught to become more aware of our emotions,' Ava says. 'Yet we aren't taught the skills to guide ourselves to our needs, desires and truths underneath. Our reliance on our emotions can mask the deeper truths within.'

In her sellout spirituality retreats and embodiment courses, Ava teaches her students around the world how self-awareness and nervous system regulation are the true tools to support us to find deep alignment, joy and success. It's the self-awareness factor that's important here: is this emotion *really* the truth?

It's not that emotions should be dismissed entirely – as our emotions are our human privilege. Emotions are our teachers – especially the uncomfortable ones. Every emotion reveals layers of hidden wisdom. Anger shows you the perimeter of your boundaries. Fear shows where your greatest power and potential resides.

And certainly, as a writer, there is nothing more powerful than capturing – through words – the raw, immediate emotion of the moment, to reflect a human experience so that you and your readers can learn something important about life. But our emotions are just one of the layers of human

The emotions are your greatest gift as a writer. They are also your cruellest enemy.

experience. As a writer, approach the layer of your emotions with curiosity rather than dependence. If you rely on your next emotional purge to produce meaningful work, this might mean that you are not open to being a healed and successful writer.

We can't sit around like junkies waiting for our next hit of an emotion in order to write something profound. That instantly makes our writing process unsustainable, and kind of *sad,* when you think about it. What we need is to have constant access to our internal well of love, where we can draw on inspiration at any time.

Write your best work when you're happy

So many writers say to me, *I can only write well when I'm sad...* Oh really? Well, what if you find more meaning *without* the rollercoaster? What if you build a life of stability and love? What if you actually *heal*? Does this mean you are no longer a writer?

True creativity is not bound by your external chaos. Your writing superpowers arise from the calm depths of a philosopher who constantly questions life and seeks truth.

Notice when you're sad: I bet it feels like your perspective is very 'short range'. And when you're happy, the world expands – right? Think about the impact this has on your writing. Staying bound by your next big burst of emotion might limit your ability to see the truth or imagine another character's perspective. If you break free from your limited world view you'll move beyond just a recount of your latest heartbreak – to crafting meaningful narratives that resonate on a universal level.

That means it's possible – more than possible – to write incredibly compelling and 'on point' pieces from a place of contentment, stability, and even happiness. So take a deep breath, blow your nose one last time, and flush the last crumbs of your emotional addiction down the toilet.

> **The magic happens when we stop clinging to our rigid views and start gathering knowledge from all corners of the world.**

Detachment creates space for truth

As I've said, in my twenties my writing felt amateur, immature, lacking. It wasn't that I had nothing to say – it was that I wasn't observing life with the right kind of *detachment*. I was too close to myself and too attached to how I thought things were meant to be.

Detachment, or *aparigraha* in Sanskrit, is a key principle in yoga and Hindu philosophy that emphasises non-attachment to possessions, desires, and outcomes. It encourages simplicity, inner freedom, and trust in the natural flow of life – letting go of the need to control or cling to things, relationships, or even personal identities. This is because true peace, happiness and clarity always comes from within.

And this goes for writing too. The magic happens when we stop clinging to our rigid views and start gathering knowledge from all corners of the world. Just like weaving a tapestry, the more threads of thought, fact, and perspective you collect, the richer and more colourful the artwork becomes.

My little story about my 2014 heartbreak? Let's just say that those years of my life were governed by instability, which I can now see with a wider lens. Now I can write about myself as a character in those days with more depth. Looking back on this scene without my desperate attachment to find love – whatever that meant for me at the time! – I can see that I was just running the same 'I'm unlovable' movie over and over again.

And in all honesty, that makes for pretty boring writing. I couldn't write about the truth, because I couldn't see that at the core of it all, I didn't love myself. I was letting my emotions run the show, and they cleverly masked what was actually underneath – a deep desire to see and honour myself. That's why *HeartWriting* starts with unlocking the loving truth of your heart, which we are going to learn more about in Part Two.

Now that I've been through truckloads of therapy, I'm writing more than ever. Actually, if I'm honest, rarely do I write my best stuff when I'm in the throes of emotion. In *On Writing: A Memoir of the Craft,* Stephen King talks about his cocaine addiction which supposedly drove his high output in his early days of his writing career.[2] He later discovered that he could write just as well without drugs: 'The idea that creative endeavor and mind-altering substances are entwined is one of the great pop-intellectual myths of our time.' And I must agree – only, my addiction is to emotions, not drugs.

Now I write with detachment – yet it's way more relatable, self-aware, and resounds with truth. It doesn't mean I'm not close to my writing, my scenes, my characters – or even the emotions I'm trying to convey. It just means that I don't have tunnel vision anymore, and I'm more aware of the reader and the relationship I am building through the text.

And I can write anytime, which is the best thing ever.

Just get the feelings out first: journalling

I always use my journal to sift through the first layer of feelings, just as Julia Cameron, author of *The Artist's Way*, says we should all do in our 'morning pages'. Now, many years after my heartbreak phase, sifting through my journals provides me with not just a few laughs, but also the missing pieces in my current stories. I have such gratitude for my notebooks, Word docs and apps filled with random thoughts, words, old letters. These snippets of thought have become a goldmine for my characters. They aren't all profound writings, but you can feel their truth at that time.

See, emotional writing isn't a total waste of time; we should all use a humble journal to get the icky feelings out. Just don't trick yourself into thinking that emotions are the only time you can write, or the only thing you can produce that is publishable. This couldn't be further than the truth! Rather, treat your journal as a daily practice. *Slow and steady wins the race.* Capture the awakenings, realisations and descriptions, moment by moment. You never know – these snippets might end up in a book one day. And that stupid boy you wrote about years ago might end up becoming a brilliant or awful character in disguise much later.

How to journal

People often ask me how I journal. I don't know. I don't have rules for journalling – although I have lots of rules for creative writing and professional editing.

Writing and journalling are two different things:

1. Writing is for (hopefully) sharing with the world.
2. Journalling is just for you.

A journal is the one place you know you won't be judged. So write the absolute truth, no matter what, because this is the first stage of healing through writing. One day you might like to reshape that journal entry into a piece of perfected, edited and publishable writing. Now that's another story for the final section of this book. For now, enjoy spilling your guts to the page, no censor required.

I don't use prompts much. I just write from my inner voice. There is no need for fancy words or sparkly language. There is only room for the truth of my heart. But, knowing that a lot of other writers do like to start with prompts, here is a list that will get you thinking and writing through the layers of your memories, senses, and truth. *The absolute truth.*

21 JOURNAL QUESTIONS FOR ABSOLUTE TRUTH

1. What was the hardest conversation you've ever had – and can you describe the entire event, including the smells, sounds, and textures around you?

2. What was the sexiest moment in your life?

3. What was the sexiest moment in your life, that wasn't sexy at all?

4. What memory do you return to the most, and why? Write about it as if you're seeing it for the first time, capturing every detail you can remember.

5. What's a moment in your life when you felt truly seen? Describe the experience and the emotions it brought up, and write it like a love letter.

6. Describe a time when you felt like you failed at something important. What did it teach you, and how did it shape you afterward?

7. Who in your life has challenged you the most? What did that relationship reveal about you?

8. Write about a time when you acted out of character. What triggered this, and how did it feel to be in that moment?

9. What's a belief or value you once held strongly that has since changed? Describe the journey that led to this transformation.

10. Describe a place that feels like home to you, but isn't. What does this place mean to you, and what memories does it carry?

11. Think of a time you kept a secret. Write about the weight of it, what it meant to carry it, and why you kept it hidden.

12. What's a song that takes you back to a vivid memory? Describe the memory as if you're reliving it, including any details about the setting and emotions.

13. Describe a time when you felt intense joy for something small. What does that moment reveal about who you are?

14. What's a part of yourself you try to hide? Write about it with compassion, as if explaining it to a trusted friend.

15. Who do you miss, and what would you say to them if you could speak openly?

16. What's the kindest thing someone has ever done for you? Reflect on how it made you feel, and why it's stayed with you.

17. What's something you know you should forgive yourself for but haven't yet? Write a letter to yourself, forgiving this part of you.

18. What's a dream or desire you rarely admit, even to yourself? Explore it here, imagining what your life might look like if it came true.

19. Think of a time when you were misunderstood. Describe the incident from your perspective and reflect on how it felt.

20. What's a piece of advice you'd give your younger self? Write it out, along with any memories that inspired this advice.

21. Write about the most beautiful moment you've witnessed that had nothing to do with you. How did it affect you?

PART TWO
Surrender

Listen to your heart

CHAPTER FIVE

The heart of the writer

Things really started to change for me when the act of writing started to become a spiritual force of love. Suddenly, I was no longer wrestling with words. Instead, I was in conversation with them: a loving relationship that had nothing to do with deadlines or recognition. 'Wow – does this have something to do with my heart?' I wondered.

Place a hand on your heart right now. Feel its energy, its knowing. Here, nestled beneath your sternum, is the divine centre where your truth and creativity truly reside. You can physically and energetically feel that everything is connected, and everything is love, when tuning in to this space.

There is a voice, isn't there? Can you hear it?

Pause. Close your eyes. Listen.

The tone has changed, hasn't it?

The voice you hear is channelling something profound from the depths of your being. These are your magic words. Your heart words. Words that touch others, ripple through history, and reshape worlds. But they are not from intellect. They emerge from the knowledge of your heart.

When we become attuned to this voice, we realise that

we have found our greatest author within. And it's not just about words. It's about synchronicities that feel like messages, moments that feel like portals. It's about opportunities appearing out of nowhere. It's about people arriving in our lives like whispers from something greater.

For me, becoming a *HeartWriter* was not just about finding the right words. It was about living from the heart. *Becoming everything my heart always wanted me to be. Listening* – not just with my ears, but with an entirely new sense of hearing.

You know this to be true, because I'm sure you've felt things that you couldn't really explain. I bet you've walked into a room and instantly sensed the energy – before anyone spoke a word. Your heart told you something – maybe you felt a sharpness in the air, or a heaviness you couldn't ignore. Or maybe you gravitated toward someone whose presence felt like warm golden light.

When you learn to attune deeply, your heart tells you yes, and your heart tells you no. This is honestly how I live my life these days – through the attunement I feel to my heart's messages. But before we go deeper, let's consider the science behind all this magic.

> **When we become attuned to this voice, we realise that we have found our greatest author within.**

Heart coherence and its role in creativity

Our hearts are scientifically quite remarkable, brimming with an inbuilt intelligence that harmonises the mind, emotions, and body, according to research from the *HeartMath* Institute.[3]

There is a powerful electromagnetic field created by your heart, which spans several feet beyond the body. This electromagnetic field is over 100 times stronger than the brain's, which is why you can sense and feel things before you consciously register them. This impacts our perception and relationships, and even influences how others perceive us. If you're feeling joyous, the world will know, and they'll feel uplifted too. If you're feeling dark and down, well – yes, that will influence the way others feel, even if you try to hide it.

Much of *HeartMath's* research centres around a concept called 'heart coherence'. Heart coherence refers to a state of synchronisation between the heart, brain, and nervous system. When our heart rhythms are erratic – when we're stressed, self-doubting, or pushing too hard – our body and mind are pulled out of alignment, and our creative pathways close like a fist. But when we enter a state of heart coherence – a smooth, balanced heart rhythm that provides harmony throughout the systems in the body – we unlock a cascade of clarity, and we can hear our internal voice and intuition once more. We are literally sharper and more intuitive when experiencing heart coherence, thanks to the powerful connection between the heart and the brain's prefrontal cortex – the thinking and reasoning centre. The heart also has a direct neural pathway to the amygdala, the emotional processing centre of the brain. This means the heart's powerful signal improves our emotional regulation, connects us to joy, and ignites creative drive and flow.

When we achieve heart coherence, our entire system synchronises. The heart's signals to the brain become smooth and rhythmic, unlocking the following benefits for writers:

- ✓ **Sharper intuition** (knowing the right path without overthinking)
- ✓ **Deeper creativity** (ideas feel like they 'arrive' rather than being forced)
- ✓ **Authentic communication** (words and relationships feel natural, heartfelt, and true)
- ✓ **Resilience** (more adaptable, less likely to give up when faced with challenges)

How can we achieve heart coherence?

We can cultivate this state whenever we embrace moments of joy, peace, and gratitude. *HeartMath* explains that the quickest route is through a minute of deep breathing and meditation. But a heart-coherent state is not just about rest and relaxation – because it's less about the speed of your heart and more about the rhythm and pattern of your heartbeat. That's why you can also be in high heart coherence when dancing, singing, or even running.

And this state is *gold* for a writer.

If you're truly ready to live a life of alignment and heart coherence, begin by recognising when you are *not* anchored in love – like when you're operating in a state of fear, pride, or 'I need to be the best.' Write down when you notice these feelings arise, and remind yourself that these are merely protective mechanisms. Then, work through the following sections one by one, followed by a deep, heart-opening meditation.

> **When writing from the heart, words become expressions of the divine within us.**

'HeartWriting' starts with love

When writing from the heart – in a state of heart coherence – words are no longer about external goals like *I want this, I have to be that*. Instead, they become expressions of the divine within us, shared with the world not out of a need for approval, but out of a deep well of internal love.

I didn't know this in my early days. Back then, I was desperate to prove myself. I crammed my writing with metaphors. I used words to impress, to convince. I wrote from the mind, not the heart. And if I'm being honest? I was terrified. Terrified of being misunderstood. I overcompensated – for fear that people wouldn't hear my ecstasy and emphasis. For *fear?* – that's not love. That's not trust. Can you hear what I'm saying here?

And now when I write – I'm more relaxed. I don't care so much what people think. I don't try so hard. My ego is gone, my heart doesn't need the validation, and *my words are more clear.* You can probably hear it now, even in these words – a shift in my voice, a kind of softness, a sigh of relief.

And that's the beauty of heart-led writing:

- It does not **grasp or force**. It flows.
- It does not need **validation**. It just is.
- It does not **beg to be loved**. It is **already whole**.

It's an absolute pleasure when we can feel the true essence of the writer – one who doesn't try so hard. And this all starts with the heart. Writing from a place of deep heart connection allows us to access words that feel *true* rather than merely impressive, and learning this was my ticket to finding my authenticity – and my *Why*.

Poets, musicians, artists, sages, and healers across centuries and cultures worldwide have always reported a mystical sense that their gifts come from a deeper place than the mind: a knowing that pulses from the heart, not as effort, but as divine flow. In these moments an artist is not just a creator – they are a vessel, a conduit for something greater – beauty, truth, love – flowing through them, asking to be shaped, sung, or set to paper. The more time spent in the silence of their heart, the more likely they are to feel a divine message flow through them.

Many ancient traditions understood this well:

- In Traditional Chinese Medicine, the heart is known as 'the seat of all knowledge', the true home of wisdom – not the mind.
- In Ancient Egypt, the heart was considered the most sacred organ, the record of a person's life, weighed against the feather of Ma'at to determine one's fate in the afterlife.
- In Indian philosophy, the heart chakra, *anahata*, is the bridge between the physical and the spiritual, governing love, compassion, and creativity – the very essence of artistic expression.

Open the heart space: anahata

In Sanskrit, *anahata* means 'unstruck sound', or the sound of the celestial realm – the resonance of something pure, untapped, waiting to be expressed. It is also known as the heart space or the heart chakra, and it is the bridge between what we know and what we feel: the intangible force that moves through us when inspiration strikes. I felt this deeply on that day in Peru, when my heart burst open and the words came – not from effort, but from surrender.

As writers, we know what it feels like when creativity stagnates, when the words don't come, or when self-doubt wraps around our minds like vines. That's a blocked heart. Fear, attachment, and unresolved emotions choke creative flow. Writing becomes something we push through, rather than something that pulls us forward.

But when *anahata* is open? Writing feels different.

- **Ideas arrive effortlessly.**
- **Words flow as if we are simply the vessel.**
- **The 'unstruck sound' of creativity moves through us.**

In Sanskrit, *anahata* means 'unstruck sound', or the sound of the celestial realm.

Unlike the lower chakras, which are tied to the body, survival and ego, or the upper chakras, which connect us to higher consciousness, *anahata* is the space that merges both realms together in grounded awareness. Everything is *felt* here, powerfully vibrating 'I love' out to the universe.

As a creative, this is the sweet spot between effort and surrender, where writing ceases to be an act of striving and becomes an act of loving devotion. So, when the words feel stuck, the problem isn't in the mind – it's in the heart. The question isn't 'How do I write better?' It's more like … 'Where am I not allowing myself to feel?'

The Buddhist heart-mind of the writer

In Buddhist philosophy, *citta*, the heart-mind, emphasises the central role of the heart in shaping our consciousness. To Buddhists, there is no divide between thinking and feeling; they rise together, shaping how we perceive the world, how we write, and how we live.

Have you ever woken up in a good mood, only to find that everything feels brighter? And on the flip side – when woken up anxious or heavy, everything around you reflects it? The world seems colder. People are distant. Even your morning coffee tastes off. That's *citta* at work. It's not just about what's happening around you – it's about how your heart is translating reality.

For writers, when the heart-mind is clouded with fear, self-doubt, or overthinking, the words feel forced. The blank page becomes an opponent rather than a canvas. But when the heart is open, light, and at ease, writing flows as naturally as breath. So how do we cultivate a clear, open heart? Buddhism offers us two essential practices, both invaluable to the writer's craft:

- **Metta (loving-kindness)**: Imagine wrapping yourself (and others) in a warm, soft blanket of compassion. Metta encourages warmth and human connection, helping us shift from judgement to kindness. Instead of fearing the blank page, we meet it like an old friend. Instead of harsh self-criticism, we write as if speaking to someone we love.

- **Vipassana (insight meditation):** This is one of the oldest forms of Buddhist meditation, often translated as 'clear seeing' or 'insight.' It's about observing reality as it is, without getting caught up in judgements, reactions, or stories about what's happening. You don't push away your thoughts – or hold onto them. You just notice:
    - *Ah, here's a wave of self-doubt ... and now it's passing.*
    - *Here's a tangled sentence ... now it's untangling itself.*
    - *Here's the urge to impress ... now it's dissolving.*

This is how we write with heartfelt presence, without being owned by our thoughts or ruled by our fears. We don't cling. We don't resist. We simply show up, open-hearted, and let the words come.

The subconscious heart of the writer

Now let's step deeper into the heart space and the psyche. Carl Jung, famous for his subconscious work, saw the heart not just as a symbol of 'feeling' but as a gateway to the depths of the psyche, where the subconscious holds both our hidden wounds and our greatest creative potential. He claimed that the more we attune ourselves to the desires of the heart – what *deeply* moves us – the more we align with our authentic nature. Much of this work happens through our imagination, dreams, and deep reflection, as we allow the gateway of the heart to swing open and reveal to us hidden truths. And when the truth is set free, creativity flows with passion, power and infinite possibility. But this comes down to our courage to embrace even the darkest chambers of the heart – often in silence and deep meditation.

Meditation for heart coherence and deep insight

In the mountains of Peru, when tears rolled like a ritual and my heart cracked wide open, essentially I was just sitting in nature meditating. I wasn't doing anything extraordinary.
I was simply sitting in stillness. I was listening.
And then the words came.
Not as thoughts, but as a voice deeper than thought:

'You need to face your fears. You need to make a life out of what you love.'

Months later, in a formal meditation practice back home, she whispered again, this time with even more clarity:

'You are going to be a professional writer. You'll travel far to become this writer. You'll enrol in a master's program, open writing workshops, and change lives. You'll teach others to write and live fearlessly, just like you.'

I rushed to my bedroom and scribbled this dessert-list of dreams into my diary. I listened to her message and clutched the pages of promises to my chest. *And all of it came true.* Two years later I became a paid writer and editor. I haven't stopped listening to my heart since.

When we meditate, we naturally and quickly shift into that state of heart coherence we spoke of earlier – a harmonious rhythm of heartbeats that enhances deep insight. But it's not just science. This is also a form of heart-led magic. Your spirit calls you to meditate, and to write: and you know this, because your heart-led words, when laid on a page, can sometimes seem to spill from some other place. When these words come along you almost can't recognise the voice. *But it's yours, and it's coming from your heart.*

The heart helps us to write hard things

Sometimes the things we are called to write require great courage. If we truly listened to the whispers of our heart, we would know that we are talented and brave enough to achieve works of beauty and brilliance – even when the content is hard or heartbreaking. We are divinely sacred beings, each of us a unique expression of genius at work in a world that desperately needs our gifts. When we embrace this truth, our work and our art becomes more than just about recognition; it becomes a devotional practice to the Self, an offering of love to the world. And often, our works pour out faster and better due to this deep reverence and surrender.

And so, I invite you: place a hand on your heart. Listen. The words are already there. They always have been. Now, write. Write the honesty, the hardship, the blood that spills from your heart without wiping the edges clean. It's through this openness that we can write our most authentic and meaningful work, and by connecting deeply with the heart, we come back to coherence and love. Fear, hate and jealousy naturally dissolve when love is activated. Writers' block fades, and we can create our most powerful words. As we write through our pain, we not only heal ourselves but also offer a path to healing for our readers.

> **When we risk cracking wide open, we hurt, and simultaneously we allow joy to flow through us too.**

When we risk cracking wide open, we hurt, and simultaneously we allow joy to flow through us too. When we are too afraid of the pain, we let neither in. So how much pain do we let in? When is enough *enough*?

You'll know: because the answer to everything is always **love**.

The heart of the writer – summary

- **Heart coherence is a measurable state that enhances creativity, intuition, and depth.** We can access this through meditation, breathwork, and emotional awareness.

- **Writing is about surrendering to truth.** When we write from the heart, we surrender, allowing truth to flow rather than forcing it.

- **The ego strives; the heart flows.** The most powerful writing does not beg to be admired. It is whole, even in its imperfection.

- **The heart has always been central to wisdom and storytelling.** Ancient cultures revered it as the seat of knowledge, and modern science confirms its intuitive power.

- **Writing from the heart requires courage.** To tell the truth, we must be willing to feel deeply, to listen, and to let go of the need for approval.

NURTURING YOUR INTUITIVE HEART THROUGH THE ELEMENTS: AIR, FIRE, EARTH, WATER.

1. **Choose an element for today:** Based on what you learned or felt about your heart today, select an element that feels supportive. If your heart feels restless, the earth element may offer stability. If it feels heavy, fire might bring energy.

2. **Write a letter to your heart, using elemental imagery:** Imagine that your heart embodies this element. Write a letter to your heart as if it were a friend, using imagery inspired by that element. For example:
   - **Air:** Describe your heart as a breeze, free and light, perhaps needing grounding to prevent drifting.
   - **Fire:** See your heart as a flame, passionate and strong, perhaps needing a bit of calm to avoid burnout.
   - **Earth:** Picture your heart as a mountain, solid and reliable, maybe in need of a little movement to shake things up.
   - **Water:** Imagine your heart as a flowing river – or perhaps the river has become still.

3. **Reflect on what surprised you today about your heart's wisdom:** Think back on anything that surprised you about your heart today – whether it was a feeling, an insight, or a response to an experience. What did this reveal about your deeper self or purpose?

After completing these exercises, take a moment to sit quietly with your hand on your heart. Breathe deeply and thank your heart for its wisdom, its support, and its friendship. End by writing a note of gratitude for your heart's unique qualities and the guidance it offered you today.

CHAPTER SIX

Spirit of the story

Latin: <u>inspīrāre</u>

Inspire.
To breathe an idea into the world.
The breath, full of life.
Ideas, born.

There's more being spoken through spirit than just words: there are magnificent *stories* flowing through you. Some of these stories are rooted in this life, while others come from past lives, ancestors, spirits, or the cosmos. It is your mission in this life to listen to these stories, write them down, and pass them on as a healing tool for the world. This is because stories are not just stories; they are magic *and* medicine, a way of making sense of existence. A way of connecting with spirit.

The sacred function of storytelling is not new – it has been recognised and honoured across cultures since the beginning of time. An example of this is the Dreaming, known by many names across First Nations communities of Australia. For the Warlpiri people of the Tanami Desert region in the Northern Territory, it is called Jukurrpa. In the Central Desert, the

Arrernte people speak of Altyerre; the Anangu Pitjantjatjara Yankunytjatjara peoples refer to Tjukurpa; and in the East Kimberley, the Kija people call it Ngarrangkarni. Though the words vary, the Dreaming is understood as a Spiritual reality that encompasses the past, present and future. It is not simply a moment in time, but a powerful Creation story and a living force that continues to guide Law, Culture and connection to Country.

Much like the ancestral stories passed down through oral traditions, the Dreaming is a living, breathing narrative – one that not only preserves Cultural knowledge but also restores Spiritual and emotional balance. Stories are sung or retold, and lessons are learned over time – gradually, with age and maturity – not when one wants or expects to see, know, or hear. When someone is unwell – physically, mentally, or emotionally – Elders or healers may guide them back to harmony through their Story. But nobody is above or below anyone else when it comes to Community, connection and Dreaming. In the same way that no single storyteller owns the truth, each person holds a responsibility to guide one another back to their roots, helping them reconnect with their Dreaming Story – a tale that might not unfold in a straight line but instead spiral through meaning over time.

Dream stories and rituals

While the Dreaming is not about dreaming in the literal, sleep-related sense, many First Nation Australians do recognise dreams as meaningful. Across various Aboriginal and Torres Strait Islander cultures, dreams may carry messages, insights or connections to Ancestors and Country. Similarly, many cultures throughout history have trusted dreams as a source of wisdom, guidance, and healing. Across the world, dream stories have served as portals to deeper understanding, shaping individual and communal knowledge for thousands of years:

- Indigenous Traditions in the Americas – Many Native American and First Nations tribes, such as the Ojibwe and Lakota, practice dream quests, where individuals seek dreams or visions as guidance from spirit guides. In these cultures, shamans (or medicine people) also often receive healing songs and rituals for their community through dreams.
- Siberian and Mongolian Shamanism – In Tuvan and Evenki shamanic traditions, dreams are considered messages from the spirit world. Shamans enter dream states to retrieve lost souls, diagnose illness, or communicate with ancestor spirits.
- Ancient Egypt – The Egyptians were obsessed with recording dreams, and employed oracles, whose job was to interpret dreams as divine messages from deities like Thoth.
- Ancient Greece – Dreams were considered a form of medicine. The Temple of Asclepius, the Greek god of healing, was a place where sick people would sleep in sacred spaces to receive visions of cures.
- Tibetan and Hindu Traditions – In Tibetan Buddhism,

dream yoga is a practice where dreams are used for spiritual awakening. In Hinduism, many sacred texts describe sages receiving divine knowledge through dreams.

Whether in the quiet of the night or the rhythm of a song, messages from the unseen world have long guided people toward truth and healing *through story*.

> **Whether in the quiet of the night or the rhythm of a song, messages from the unseen world have long guided people toward truth and healing *through story*.**

Shamanic storytelling

In many ancient societies, storytellers and healers were one and the same. Shamans, known as the keepers of the original lore, were the guardians of cultural memory and spiritual wisdom. Storytelling was not just a way to teach; it was a means of connection, healing, and transformation, bridging gaps between self and others, between generations, between seen and unseen realms.

A shamanic journey is, in essence, a journey through story – sometimes through dreams, sometimes through imagination or visions. The shaman enters trance states, moving between worlds to locate information that could heal or guide their community. Through the shaman's journey, they bring back a gift, an insight, a truth. The wisdom they retrieve comes not in the form of direct answers, but through symbols, archetypes, and memories that speak to the deeper layers of the unconscious. This mirrors Joseph Campbell's concept of the Hero's Journey – a cycle of descent, discovery, and return.

The role of the modern storyteller

The role of the shaman-storyteller has not disappeared. If anything, it is needed more than ever. We may have lost our way from ancient wisdom and the mythic past, but the role of the shaman has been lovingly passed down by our shamanic brothers and sisters to you and me. Now *we* are the spiritual storytellers, making meaning through language, travelling to other dimensions of reality, interpreting dreams, and using the insights of imagination to create new visions rooted in ancient wisdom.

And, like the storytellers before us, we write.

Not just to tell stories, but to make meaning. To restore connection. To carry forward the wisdom that is, and always has been, flowing through us.

Inspīrāre: To breathe an idea into the world

So where on earth did the first dream come from? Dreams are the ultimate mystery. Imagine this: the first human dream was essentially *a brand-new story* breathed into the dreamer's consciousness, something never actually experienced in the waking world. This dream was shared with others around the campfire, and in doing so, a new story entered the collective consciousness. Was it fiction? The subconscious? Or was it the spiritual world at work?

The word *inspiration* comes from the Latin word *inspīrāre*, meaning 'to breathe in' or 'to breathe upon.' The Greeks first believed that inspiration came from the muses, divine beings who would breathe an idea into the minds of loyal human followers so that these ideas could manifest on Earth.

William Blake was a famous 19th century artist and writer who was clearly touched by the divine ideas of spirit and the power of dreams. He believed that the act of creation was not just an intellectual exercise but a conversation with God, often creating otherworldly stories, mythical creatures, and biblical allusions that flowed through him unconsciously. His deep spiritual insights can be witnessed through his many artworks, poetry, and pieces of music he created over the 19th century.

Carl Jung also believed deeply in the healing powers of story, and particularly loved William Blake's work. The early 20th century Swiss psychiatrist said that the journey toward individuation – the process of becoming whole – requires us to dive into the darkest depths of our being, through the process of making art. Jung described our shadows to be the parts of ourselves we have buried deep within our psyche. Far from being obstacles, these shadows are doorways to our most profound healing and creativity – once we open the door.

> 'There is only one way and that is your way.'
> – *Carl Gustav Jung*, The Red Book

Jung often wrote, painted, or crafted during times of emotional distress or meditation. And he knew there was something magical in dreams, just like the ancient shamans did. He believed strongly in the collective consciousness: *my dreams are connected to your dreams; my stories are connected to your stories.*

When you think about it, it's incredible that us humans are bestowed with the gift of imagination. That's what sets us apart, and that explains why the creative path is inherently a spiritual path, and vice versa: one that requires us to engage with the full spectrum of human and cosmic experience. The problem is that spiritual work – and writing – is not always *easy* or *fun* work, because of all those damn shadows that Jung always talked about.

REMINDER

There is something so pure, so unconscious, in the spirit codes of dreams – I encourage you to write them down as much as possible, and then later shape them into a more cohesive story. Inspiration is being breathed into you.

Spirituality and shadow work

In our new age Western 'wellness' world, spirituality is often misinterpreted as something cute, trendy and therapeutic – crystals, massage, affirmations, plant medicine, breathwork – sometimes without an understanding of the cultural lineages these practices emerge from. This can lead to unconscious appropriation or misrepresentation of sacred traditions. While rituals can construct a beautiful experience (that I used to seek like a drug addict during times of turmoil) unfortunately they can also act as a sweetly pleasant bypass, or a process of seeking answers externally: distractions from the deep, painful silence required for sitting with the self in shadow work.

What spirituality practice feels right for you? No judgement here, because I've toyed with most spiritual or wellness modalities on my quest for healing. Ten years ago I dove into the healing powers of crystals. It felt good to focus on the meaning of each stone rather that shine the light inward. I also taught yoga as a method of avoiding myself. To my clients, I acted like an Indian guru who knew the meaning of life – which I'm not, and I don't. I also went *hard* down the road of herbal medicine, desperate to find the plant that would heal my tummy pains, which I now realise was my way of not wanting to face what was *really* going on. Yes, a heap of external seeking and bypassing. Luckily I had some very good mentors who steered me in the right path, and encouraged me to do two things:

1. Get very still.
2. Ask more questions.

So what exactly is spirituality?

Spirituality is not about blind belief in a teacher, a set of mantras, or a list of remedies. It's about deep self-connection. Self-knowing. The realisation that your inner spirit is connected to a greater spirit. The ability to question – not out of doubt, but to deepen your understanding. The desire to tune in to the most authentic voice inside. No longer seeking externally, you listen within and shape your own belief systems. If something doesn't feel right, it's good to ask why.

I was brought up Catholic, and from a young age I found myself questioning the teachings of the Church. It wasn't that I didn't respect my parents, the priest, or the people. I liked going to church – mostly to see my friends – and I loved the singalongs. But I was always suspicious of the patriarchy of the Church, and I didn't like being told what to do, or how to feel worthy. Some things in religion just didn't sit well with me. So, one day, I came up with my own belief system: *'Just be a good person, and keep an open mind.'*

So what does it mean to 'be spiritual' – and what does it have to do with your writing? Well, spirituality is the deep and often personal experience of connection – to self, others, and the universe. It is an

> **Spirituality is not about blind belief in a teacher, a set of mantras, or a list of remedies. It's about deep self-connection.**

ongoing inquiry into meaning, purpose, and existence, guided by a sense of wonder, reverence, or inner knowing. Spirituality is less about dogmatic belief and more about your evolving relationship with the mysteries of existence, often involving rituals like meditation, contemplation, or creative acts *like writing*. Even the simple act of asking questions is a spiritual practice – especially for a curious, heart-led writer like me.

As I've grown older, I've realised I've become a *Hopeful Skeptic*, in the words of Jamil Zaki, a psychologist at Stanford University. I ask a lot of questions. I keep an open mind. I research both sides. I don't jump to conclusions. I respect that there could be more than one truth out there. I'm open to shifting my beliefs, and I definitely don't bathe my crystals in moonlight anymore. This sense of openness, combined with critical discernment, is also deeply connected to my skills as a writer: my ability to research, ponder diverse perspectives, and approach my work with careful consideration, humility, and sensitivity.

I now sense there's a force greater than us, stories breathed into existence as if by some unseen hand. That means I believe in God, right? What this force looks like, I have no idea –but I feel it, and I realise that's what Jesus was talking about, too. Perhaps, after all, there are a few truths scattered through the Bible. And perhaps our writing is a more spiritual calling than I ever dared to believe.

But, dear writer, you don't need all the answers

So many writers come to me wanting to write a self-help book that attempts to answer all the questions, usually to position them as a thought leader. But spiritually, and truthfully, you can't have all the answers. You are an equal part of a greater whole, with infinite truths to be found in the cosmos. You are simply part of the collective consciousness, writing words to represent an idea or vision that has erupted from your soul to be shared. And what is more important is that you are deeply connected to self, spirit, and the world to encourage *inspiration*.

Just like an artist, all you can do is refine your craft, and offer a representation of life through words. The key word here is *representation*.

Breathing spiritual truth into your work

The most powerful writing allows the reader to glean *their own answers* from the shades of meaning that have been painted in the prose. OK, I'm about to get my English teacher hat on, so grab your highlighters.

Meaning in a piece of writing is always dependent on *context*: that means that the reader's role is just as important as yours (the writer's). We cannot trust any text to be the absolute truth, because every text is biased, even when attempting to be unbiased:

- Dictionary definitions are based on one authority's interpretation in a particular time and place: and most definitions, up until the last fifty years, were penned by rich white men. Is that 'truth'?
- Each dictionary edition is slightly different as the lexicon evolves over the years. What is more correct – the definition of the word two centuries ago, or the meaning of the word today? And how about new words that get 'made up'?
- History books are full of false information, and ancient texts like the Bible have been rewritten countless times. By whom? For what purpose and effect?

Context affects the way we make meaning. Sure, each reader will *infer* meaning based on what has been *implied*, but they will also *contribute* meaning when the text conjures memories and ideas based on their own experiences – and ancestors' experiences – of life. The audience of Shakespeare in the 16th Century understood the meaning of a Shakespeare play very differently to today's audience.

So, as a writer, it's important to let go of your intended outcome – in the same way that Shakespeare could never have predicted that his texts would one day be critiqued through a neo-feminist lens. It is the gifted writer who steps back from their ego to be 'right' and allows their reader space to feel and breathe, as if they are divinely one with the text.

Your 'real role' as a spiritual writer

What has all this got to do with spirituality? Well, everything. Because now you are going to step back – zoom out – and look at how your world and your spirituality has shaped your context, your knowledge, and your calling as a writer. Your writing is not here to indoctrinate.

> **This chapter is the result of my surrender to a greater knowing, a divine message, and a deep respect to you, the reader.**

Absolute truth – if it exists – transcends human concepts and language. We can approach it, glimpse it, and attempt to write about it, but our day-to-day understanding remains a reflection of our own lens. I also had to learn this lesson, too, in the shaping of this book. Before I knew it, the writing was taking on a life of its own, and this chapter is the result of my surrender to a greater knowing, a divine message, and a deep respect to you, the reader, in allowing you to take what you need from these words.

Even if you feel that you have received a message of truth from spirit, all you can do is write it down. Perhaps you will open hearts. Perhaps you will expand possibilities. But you can't be attached to the outcome. You're simply sharing a message and a gift – through your lens, and through language. Depending on how you write this story, it can help and heal others. It can influence lasting change. *Gently. Subtly. Skilfully.* But the first step is to let go of your need to be right, and see what spiritually shines through.

Later in this book, but mostly in my workshops, you'll learn about some of the techniques that can help you skilfully shape a dream or a journal entry into a beautifully-structured text for purpose, meaning, audience and effect – something that I taught at university entrance exam level for many years. Technique is not separate from your spiritual work – it enhances the reverence and thoughtfulness in your ideas and craft. I've always loved arming my students with loads of tools in their toolbox, because it allows them freedom to shape their vision – in the same way an artist armed with better brushes and techniques creates a sharper, more otherworldly painting. Technique works perfectly alongside spirit: it allows writers to be more thoughtful, to write and read from all angles, to check you aren't just telling people what to do and how to think, but rather, invite a vision, and a feeling – and then let go of the desired outcome, because once that story is out of your hands, it no longer has anything to do with you.

And so, now *you* have made a creative and spiritual offering to the world. This is the most beautiful part of being a writer – once you have overcome all your fears of failure, and you learn that this thing is greater than you, it's far easier to offer your gift up to the world just like throwing an offering into a blazing Vedic fire ceremony: *Here. My words are for the world.*

Just like throwing an offering into a
blazing Vedic fire ceremony:
Here. My words are for the world.

We are modern day shamans of the story

Several years ago, a psychic told me that I had roots in shamanism. At the time, I didn't fully understand the role of shamans, even after visiting the shaman statues in South America. I just kind of giggled. *OK. Cool. I'm a shaman, whatever that means,* I thought to myself, half in disbelief. Now I see entirely through the lens of shamanism. My role in *HeartWriting* is to continue the tradition of meaningful storytelling that can create positive change for others.

In my classes, it's undeniable that shamanic magic happens. I witness writers opening like a flower, and crying at their heart-wrenching words – and at others'. I've come to realise that everyone's story is unique and written for an important reason. It's spellbinding to witness someone 'falling apart' over their writing: those words that shake you down like a tree full of fat rain drops – and leave your branches bare with vulnerability. You're stunned, and we're stunned too – because you've stumbled on something unique, something so true, in your writing.

As you continue your writing journey, remember that your words have the power to heal, transform, and inspire. Whether you're writing for yourself, for others, or for the whole world, know that your voice is a pure force of magic and light. So, take a breath. *You don't need to know it all.* Let spirit breathe the life and meaning into your words.

Spirit of the story: a summary

1. **Storytelling has always been a sacred act, deeply connected to healing and wisdom.** In ancient societies, shamans were both storytellers and healers, using narrative to bridge gaps between worlds, generations, and cultures.

2. **Stories are not just entertainment; they are medicine.** They help us heal, understand ourselves, and make sense of existence. When we write, we contribute to a timeless tradition of storytelling as a tool for transformation.

3. **Shamanic storytelling is a form of spiritual exploration.** Through trance and altered states, shamans retrieved insights from the unconscious – much like writers today, who draw from memory, archetypes, and imagination to craft meaningful stories.

4. **Inspiration is not owned; it is received.** The word 'inspiration' comes from the Latin *inspīrāre*, meaning 'to breathe in.' Just as ancient cultures believed ideas were gifted by divine forces, writers must surrender to the flow of creativity rather than force control over it.

5. **Great writing requires letting go of ego.** Writers cannot dictate how their work will be received – just as Shakespeare couldn't have foreseen his plays being critiqued through modern lenses. A skilled writer creates space for the reader to interpret and engage.

6. **Spirituality and storytelling both require openness and questioning.** True self-knowledge is not found in blind belief but in a willingness to ask, explore, and remain receptive to different perspectives and possibilities.

7. **The writer's calling is to listen, translate, and share.** Whether stories arise from personal experience, ancestral wisdom, or universal consciousness, our task is to honour them, continuing the lineage of storytelling as a sacred and healing practice.

8. **Modern writers inherit the role of the shaman.** In a world disconnected from ancestral traditions, writers serve as the new spiritual storytellers – interpreting dreams, channelling wisdom, and using language to reconnect people with deeper truths.

EXERCISES TO INVITE SPIRIT

1. How has the process of reading and writing created spiritual healing in your life?

2. As a writer, are you willing to invite spirit in, to explore and write about what others are not willing to see?

3. Create a fiction story with a central theme about 'healing through the power of words'.

Once you've completed your work, share it with others. You can post it on the *HeartWriting Community Group* on Facebook or share it with a trusted friend or writing circle. Go on, be the shaman of the story.

CHAPTER SEVEN

Silence, meditation, movement

My true superpowers as a writer started to bloom when I learned to embrace silence. My best words have always arisen from times of stillness, like that magical day in the countryside of Peru: tears falling and wonder rising.

Years before Peru, I was a young, fiery, overworked teacher. I had poor self-esteem, little self-awareness, and I was actively avoiding my dreams. But the real catalyst of transformation was when I hurt my back and I could barely walk into work.

I enrolled in my first yoga class on the advice of my physio. But I'd only signed up for the stretching, not the soul-searching. As I lay down for savasana, aching from a sequence of gruelling stretches, I exhaled with audible relief as the teacher's voice gently guided us to relax and visualise white fluffy clouds passing by our minds. 'When a thought comes by – just let it float gently past your mind, like the clouds,' he whispered. The incense and his words engulfed me. This was years before my travels, years before my *HeartWriting* vision, years before I knew this would be my life.

I frowned, deeply focused on pushing aside fluffy clouds.

OK – I think I get it – yes – this is nice. Suddenly something inside me built up like a great roar – and then – *Poof* – all that cataclysmic energy was snuffed out, and a deep, otherworldly connection within my heart bloomed. Slowly, softly, subtly. Tears began to pour as I experienced my very first spiritual awakening, a moment which felt like pure glittering magic raining down on me: yes, *that* was the moment that lovingly anchored me into a life of meditation.

This was also the turning point which prompted me to blow up my life, leave my marriage, quit my job, and travel the world. I mean, all this happened a few years later, but I owe everything to that experience which 'woke me up'. I will never, *ever* forget that yoga hall, that wonderful teacher, and that particular brand of incense.

What I discovered is that I had to let go of what I thought I wanted and surrender to the truth found in the *now*.

What I discovered, in the stillness of meditation, is that I had to let go of what I thought I wanted and surrender to the truth found in the *now*. Only in the here and the now could I see not just the clouds, but past the clouds – to the inner knowledge I'd been avoiding all along.

With regular meditation I started to rewire my neural pathways, breaking the old patterns of doubt and distraction. My focus and my mission became clearer. I was able to pull myself out of self-sabotage faster (think about my moment in Peru some years later). I found the fertile ground where my most profound ideas could take root and grow (think about my novel idea coming to life on that bus).

Meditation has become my life, and my creative life-*saver*. So, why wouldn't you also be making the most of this, as a writer?

The journey into deeper meditation

After that first deep meditation, I became hooked on yoga – not so much for the physical practice (let's be honest, I was not great at touching my toes!) but for the mental and spiritual bliss that deepened with each session. After my travels and mini-awakenings, I got very serious about learning more. I enrolled in a Transcendental Meditation course, a well-known program founded by the Indian teacher Maharishi Mahesh Yogi. Though it has since grown into a highly commercialised global organisation with TM centres in most cities, this course was instrumental for my development. I also received a personalised mantra to anchor my focus.

But it wasn't until I discovered an Australian school called Functional Spirituality that my practice evolved from amateur to something more expert. I've already mentioned its founder, Ava Irani, in previous chapters. Ava taught me how to meditate deeply *on my own* without needing external guidance – or even my mantra. The mentorship with her at Functional Spirituality filled in the gaps, and I found myself moving away from external-driven modalities, instead tuning into a deep knowing within – my inner spirit, my writing, and my heart.

Meditation and flow state theory for creativity

Even if you're not spiritual, it's a great idea for any writer to learn meditation, as it's the ultimate catalyst for creative flow. Back in the 70s, Mihaly Csikszentmihalyi first wrote about flow theory in his academic papers before producing various books on the topic, including his seminal title, *Flow: The Psychology of Optimal Experience*. In his work he explored how individuals can achieve creative insight and optimal performance during deep immersion activities.

There is an abundance of research since Csikszentmihalyi's work that has strengthened a more specific link between flow theory and *meditation* – and even the role of the brainwaves. Meditation and mindfulness can influence alpha brainwave rhythms, which are associated with states of relaxed alertness conducive to flow. Artists, writers, and other creative professionals often enter these states naturally due to flow theory, but meditation offers a fast and reliable method to access this powerful creative zone regularly and reliably.

It's a perfect circle: Meditate more, create more. Create more, flow more. Flow more, and you'll probably feel like meditating more. Meditate more, and you'll create more ...

The creative brainwaves: let's go deeper

Remember how astoundingly creative you were as a child? That's because you were naturally frolicking in the dreamy alpha and theta brainwaves – the meditation brainwaves – right up until you were 11 or 12 years old.

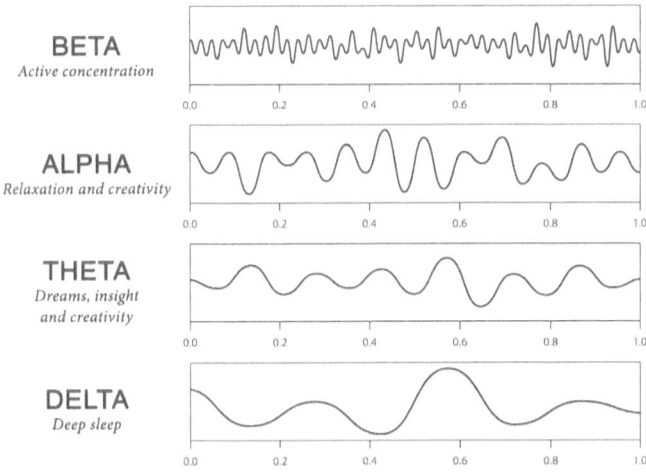

The brainwaves and their benefits. Source: Shutterstock.

Childhood is a natural cocktail of creativity, dreaminess, and joy. Around age 12 is the age when the 'smart' beta brainwave clicks in – and you find yourself pursuing goals and passing tests with higher speed and success. That's also when you lose the frequency of your high-flow state and you stop creating all those wonderful and wild things you were obsessed with when you were young. And then – you become a teenager. An adult. Beta brainwaves dominate. Life gets speedier yet harder. We are taught in modern society to push ourselves beyond our capacity. No longer do we sit around campfires like our predecessors or roll around in the grass looking at clouds after lunch. Suddenly, as high-functioning adults, we find it hard to access our dreamlike imagination of the theta brainwave, unless we are sleeping. All day long we're literally 'too much in our heads', disconnected from our hearts, and not experiencing the spaciousness of our creative subconscious.

The fastest solution? Of course. Meditation.

Thomas Edison's big secret: meditation

It turns out Thomas Edison, the famous inventor behind the light bulb, was practising meditation all along – perhaps without realising it. He would settle into a chair, holding a small steel ball in his hand. He'd then rest with eyes closed … and as he began to nod off, the ball would eventually slip from his grasp and clatter to the floor, waking him up. Right at that moment he would be struck by flashes of insight – those 'aha!' moments we all crave. He had entered the hypnagogic state – the dreamy phase between wakefulness and sleep – during which creative insights are more likely to occur. This is also known as the theta brainwave state, where the mind drifts freely from the rigid rules of conscious thought. So *this* is how Edison stumbled upon some of his greatest ideas. Scientists *can* meditate, after all.

Get silent, get smarter: meditation and the brain

Remember our talk on dopamine addiction? Studies have shown that this constant barrage of distractions doesn't just steal our time – it actively stunts and destroys our brain's capacity to think deeply and create meaningfully (ol' Thomas Edison certainly didn't have a smartphone in his pocket in the 1800s).

When we succumb to the lure of instant gratification – the constant ping of our phone – we're feeding our brains a steady diet of dopamine, the 'feel-good' neurotransmitter that lights up our reward circuits. While a little dopamine is a dash of spice in the soup of life, too much of it, especially in the form of digital distraction, can lead to addiction.

Just as distraction weakens our mental muscles, meditation strengthens them, cultivating focus, clarity, and calm. And it's not just theoretical – it's structural. Neuroscientists have found that regular meditation can increase the size and function of the prefrontal cortex and hippocampus, the regions responsible for higher-order thinking, creativity, memory, and impulse control. At the same time, activity in the brain's Default Mode Network (DMN) – which is associated with mind-wandering – tends to decrease, while regions linked to executive function and emotional regulation become more active. This shift enhances generative thinking, encourages solution-based problem-solving, and nurtures courage and resilience in the face of setbacks – all essential ingredients in the creative process.

The link between the brain and the heart

For these cognitive benefits to fully take effect, the brain and the heart must work in harmony. The heart is more than just a pump; it's a powerful regulator of the nervous system, sending signals that directly influence brain function.

Meditation activates heart coherence, and heart coherence, in turn, enhances brain function, optimising cognitive clarity and emotional resilience. The two are inextricably linked: a well-regulated heart steadies the brain, and an optimised brain sustains heart coherence. True mental and emotional wellbeing is experienced when both systems are in sync, reinforcing one another in a continuous cycle of balance, coherence, and clarity.

Just ten minutes of daily mindfulness meditation can significantly improve attention, wellbeing and creativity, while decreasing the brain's susceptibility to distraction. I can vouch for this – it's worked miracles on me. But meditation isn't the only way to achieve this state. Heart coherence (and meditative states) can also be activated through slow, rhythmic breathing, deep feelings of gratitude and love, meaningful social connection, listening to calming music, singing or chanting, spending time in nature, and even simple acts of mindfulness like journalling or being fully present. When the heart enters this harmonious state, it sends powerful signals to the brain, optimising cognitive clarity, enhancing emotional resilience, and fostering creativity and deep focus.

Phew – have I lost you yet? I hope not – because this is all pretty fascinating stuff.

Finding santosha: deep peace

OK, so we've learned that meditation is great – but it's not always easy. Some people are spooked by the unfamiliar nature of silence, especially in our noisy modern world. Me too – when I was a young adult I hated silence. And I *really* hated being alone. But once I had a few of those life-changing meditative experiences, I felt moved to practise it regularly. I got used to the perfection of peace, and it became the cornerstone of my life. Now I don't make many plans, I avoid drama, and I notice the chaos of commercial news. I'm more peaceful and reflective, even when I'm not meditating. Deeper and more lasting than any fleeting dopamine high, the ancient yogis called this state *santosha*, a Sanskrit term for deep contentment and acceptance of the present moment.

By integrating *santosha* with *advaita vedanta*, the non-dual theory of eastern spirituality, we begin to experience mind-body-spirit union. Advaita, which means 'not two' in Sanskrit, teaches that *we are one with everything*. We are not separate from our spirit. And we are not separate from the world. The individual self and the universal self are one and the same. Isn't that crazy, and beautiful, to truly realise that we are all connected?

My fave routine: meditation and morning pages

Subconscious writing *after meditation* was the start for me, just as subconscious ideas were the start for Thomas Edison.

This approach is backed by modern experts who recognise the power of the theta state for creativity and problem-solving. In her book *The Artist's Way*, Julia Cameron talks about 'morning pages,' a practice of writing stream-of-consciousness first thing in the morning, or after meditation. Cameron's theory is that we write in partnership with a greater consciousness, which is also linked to the deepest parts of oneself. By cultivating heart coherence and slowing down our brainwaves through meditation, we open the door to a richer, more imaginative inner world.

Movement is also a form of meditation for creatives

Have you ever noticed the brilliance of ideas you receive after an hour of exercise? Mindful movement, such as yoga, enhances the heart, strengthens our mind-body-spirit connection, bolsters intuition, and stimulates and balances the energy centres: all of which can significantly boost our creative potential. By aligning our physical movements with our breath and energy flow, we create a more integrated and harmonious state of being. *Asana*, or yoga postures, are the third of the eight limbs of Patanjali's Yoga Sutras.

The eight limbs of Patanjali's Yoga Sutras are:
1. *Yamas* (abstinences, or self-regulating behaviours)
2. *Niyamas* (observances, or personal discipline)
3. *Asana* (body postures to distract the mind and encourage calm)

4. *Pranayama* (breath/ life force regulation)
5. *Pratyahara* (withdrawing the outer world senses)
6. *Dharana* (one-pointed focus, concentration, flow state)
7. *Dhyana* (deep meditation)
8. *Samadhi* (mind-body integration, union of the self, transcendence)

The Yoga Sutras: the true origins of yoga

Yoga means 'yoke' – the deepest centre of connection. More than two millennia ago, yoga theory blossomed into a tradition that harmonises body, mind, and spirit – mostly through meditation and breathwork. Patanjali's Yoga Sutras, written over 2,000 years ago, are not just manuals for physical postures but are ancient guides to understanding the mind, consciousness, and creativity.

The Sutras teach that yoga is not about nailing your downward facing dog – it's about attaining a pure and present state of consciousness. You might be surprised to learn that the physical postures (asana) that dominate yoga classes today only emerged in their current form in the late 19th and early 20th centuries. Inspired in part by Swedish gymnastics, in the late 1800s the British introduced physical training into Indian boys' schools to instil discipline and improve fitness. Yoga then evolved into a more global, dynamic, posture-based discipline around 100 years ago, influenced by colonialism, capitalism, and the rise of fitness culture, with pioneers like Krishnamacharya blending these influences with traditional

Hatha yoga. This led to the development of modern styles such as Vinyasa, Iyengar, and Ashtanga. Today, yoga is often practiced as a physical exercise, but its deeper roots in pranayama, meditation, and *samadhi* remain at the heart of its true purpose.

The phrase 'sthira sukham asanam' translates to 'steady and comfortable,' reminding us that ancient yoga was more about meditative stillness than physical prowess – and this is so helpful if we are learning to become writers. Think about the rollercoaster of emotions that you experience daily, that often block your ability to write, or hide the truth from your writing – like me when I was an emotional and overworked teacher. These unsteady parts of ourselves have been shaped by external forces, preventing us from living in freedom. For example, we are *taught* to strive towards competence and success – whatever that means in our society. We are *taught* to fear being anything less. We are *taught* that writers can't 'make it.' But these are just masks from the truth, and the truth is we are connected to the whole universe, we are deeply loved simply for existing, and we are pure creative magnificence *already*, in this moment. We just need to get steady to hear the truth, and yoga helps us achieve this.

But the physical practice of yoga has its place

Gentle exercise – including yoga flow – activates the body's natural rhythms, enhances heart coherence, stimulates the release of endorphins, reduces stress, enhances mental clarity, and fosters a deep sense of body-mind connection. According to Ayurveda, movement before meditation helps clear emotional blockages along the nadis (energy channels), particularly within the chakra system: the seven major energy centres that correspond to different aspects of our physical, emotional, and spiritual wellbeing. When these chakras are open and balanced, we experience a profound sense of harmony within ourselves, allowing our creativity and inner wisdom to flow freely. Like a moving meditation, when moving our bodies in alignment with our breath we can dissolve blockages and reconnect with our natural state of being.

B.K.S. Iyengar was the founder of Iyengar Yoga: a functional approach to yoga that uses lots of assistance, props and straps to ensure that the practice is safe for all bodies. Throughout his life he committed to practising asanas for three hours a day and pranayama (breathwork) for one hour. Even at age 90 he was flipping his body into headstands – for half an hour!

Sacral chakra: the flowing waters of creativity

Here's why I *really* love the physical practice of yoga. Writers tend to stick to a sedentary life, which can lead to stagnation and depression. But the sacral chakra (*svadhisthana*) is all about flow. It's the energetic river of creativity and passion. Located in the lower abdomen, just below the navel, it governs not only our artistic expression but also our ability to experience pleasure, spontaneity, and depth. The currents of *svadhisthana* are thought to purify the deep and murky places in life – a renewing, cleansing energy.

When this chakra is open and balanced, creativity flows effortlessly like a river, and we feel like that river – inspired, connected, full of vitality. But writers sit all day long, hunched and compressed in this area – often stressed, worrying, doubting. Flow is physically blocked. The sacral powerhouse of creativity becomes stagnant. Perhaps, like me, you've struggled with pain in this area – and this is exacerbated from spending long hours sitting and engaging in intellectual, upper-body-focused work. It's a terrible cycle, because when this happens we experience creative blocks, self-doubt, depression, or emotional numbness. The secret to sacral success? Besides working on our energy and traumas ... we need to *move*, a lot more than we think we do. This is because *svadhisthana* thrives on fluidity, motion, and feeling, rather than rigid structure or overthinking.

How to unblock the sacral chakra and restore creative flow

Get moving! The sacral chakra is associated with water, symbolising flow, adaptability and change. Engage in fluid, mindful movement – such as dance, yoga, or even gentle hip circles – to help release blockages and restore flow.

- Hip-opening yoga poses (like pigeon pose, goddess pose, or baddha konasana) to unlock stored tension.
- Freeform movement or dance – letting the body move instinctively to shake off creative resistance.
- Breathwork (pranayama) – deep belly breathing stimulates the lower chakras and re-energises the mind.
- Spending time near water – bathing, swimming, or even listening to the sound of flowing water can help restore emotional and creative balance.
- Sensory play – engaging with textures, colours, and scents can stimulate svadhisthana flow. Writers might find inspiration in painting, cooking, or working with clay – activities that bypass the rational mind and awaken the senses.

And ... soon the sun comes out

Located under the heart and just above the sacral is our solar plexus: our creative inner sun. In Sanskrit this chakra is called *manipura*: meaning city of jewels. This is the energy centre that is most aligned to creative motivation and *drive* (as opposed to fear) and is embedded into the *HeartWriting* brand for this reason. As your sacral river starts flowing again, your solar plexus (inner sunshine) is needed to shift your ideas onto paper – or they'll evaporate into the sky.

The key is to engage in movement that ignites your inner light while preparing you to slow down and write: *steady and comfortable*, as the Yoga Sutras teach us. Traditional Chinese Medicine can play a role in how we bolster our inner sunshine, too. When our meridians, or energy pathways are clear, we feel more motivated, inspired, and aligned. Try Qi Gong – a powerful yet gentle practice for igniting our inner jewels while balancing our entire system. Or perhaps you'd like to try core building exercises, planks, or the breath of fire to generate warmth in your solar area.

But be careful – we don't want too much sun (too much heat). Most eastern practices integrate a Yin/Yang – Ha/Tha – Sun/Moon approach, which is all about the benefits of balance. While high-impact sports can be great for endorphins and cardiovascular health, they also increase cortisol levels, which can heighten stress. For this reason, it's important to balance fast-paced activities with slower, more mindful movement practices. A deep walk, stretch, or dance can promote a quiet, sacred knowing within the body, allowing us to connect more deeply with our inner selves, release blocked energy, and awaken our Kundalini potential.

The seven chakras. Source: Shutterstock

Kundalini Energy

Kundalini is the divine cosmic feminine energy often depicted as a coiled serpent at the base of the spine. Kundalini energy represents the creative force of the universe: a powerhouse of potential for writers. Most of us living a human existence – with all the shadows and shame built up due to our conditioning and traumas – experience frequent blockages, in particular of the heart chakra (*anahata*) and the third eye chakra (*ajna*). These blockages, often referred to as the 'dark night of the soul', can be deeply unsettling (and are often the cause of writers' block) yet they offer profound opportunities for growth and transformation.

We can use our sacred movement, meditation and breathwork practices to clear the stagnant energy and blockages that may be in the way of allowing Kundalini energy to rise from the curled-up base of our spine, clearing our passages of divine creativity. Like a wise snake, when awakened it rises through the chakras, unblocking each energy centre along the way, providing deep insight and universal wisdom and connection for the creative. Once Kundalini energy reaches the crown chakra and beyond, it is believed to lead to spiritual enlightenment.

I'll be honest – a full Kundalini awakening happens just once in a lifetime, if it happens – and it's a very rare experience, often reserved for the likes of monks that meditate in silence and solitude for fifteen years. But we can all benefit from practices that open our energy centres. By engaging in sacred movement, we can help remove energy blockages that may be linked to creative blocks or challenges in our lives, allowing our light to shine brightly in our creative work and beyond.

Tuning in to your creative genius

Now that you've been gifted a pile of great information and tools, hopefully you can see that it's easier than you once thought to ignite the ultimate creative genius in you. Just like Edison: give yourself time to rest and simply 'be'. Meditate and move mindfully every day. When you give yourself time to be slower, soft, flowing and loving, your heart opens, your mental blocks disappear, and brain function sharpens – perfect for putting your creative plans into action. You can shift your energy and clear the clutter from the top layer of your consciousness. This will help you get closely attuned with the callings of your heart: the seat of all knowledge. From there, creative magic can happen – revealing worlds and ideas you've never dreamed of.

Meditation is everywhere

Once I started meditating, everything became meditation for me. Travel. Exploring the underwater. Walking in the forest. Dancing. Watching birds. Drawing. And of course – writing. All these mindful activities were amplified when I made time each day to sit in formal meditation with no distractions or excuses. Here, deep in meditation, I could finally understand what my heart was saying all along. And now all the dots started connecting.

Now I think of my whole life like a meditation, even the mediocre moments, because I've lost all that old anger, drama and emotion I used to carry around. It doesn't matter if my mind wanders during meditation. I just do it anyway. Some days will be full of monkey mind – or bursting with big ideas. Other days are uneventful – and even boring. There's benefit no matter what, but the more I do it, the more I experience peace in everything I do. Meditation has inspired me to see the truth and beauty in every corner. I write with ease. I feel truly free.

When all else fails, all you need to do is remember how free you felt as a child: that blissful feeling when your heart would explode at the little things. Because we were so great at meditating *and moving* when we were young. We knew innately that true happiness is always about the simple joys of being alive. We just forget this when we grow up, so this book is your loving reminder.

MEDITATION EXERCISES

Right now, place a hand to your heart. Take a deep breath. Notice how connected you are to the spaces all around you. Notice your breath merging and mixing with the air. Realise that you are not separate from anything around you, and by the same token, your creativity is also not separate from you, or from anything else. Watch your creativity unfurling like the flower, naturally and effortlessly, as you align with your true nature, and the nature of the universe around you.

Next, listen to my podcast, 'Meditation for Creativity,' and write down your experience afterwards, or use these prompts to guide you.

1. **Focused attention.** This is just the start – an image, the breath, a mantra. Another tip is yoga's 'alternate nostril breathing' which can balance the activity of the two brain hemispheres, by blocking one nostril and breathing through the other, then switching.

2. **Relaxed breathing.** Try counting 6 beats in and 6 beats out until your breathing relaxes into something slow and soft.

3. **A quiet, comfortable setting with a timer for 20 mins.** Don't try to meditate at work or with your kids around. Put some headphones in, go for a walk, sit in nature, and join my guided meditations on my podcast to help block out the world. Don't open your eyes until that timer has gone off. Notice how different you feel.

4. **Detachment from Outcome:** Silently remind yourself, 'I am not attached to any outcome.' This affirmation helps release the 'yang' or active energy that may push you toward productivity or results in your writing.

5. **Image Meditation:** Choose an image that inspires you (it could be a scene in nature, a symbol, or something abstract). Close your eyes and visualise this image, bringing it into your mind as vividly as possible. After meditating, open your journal and describe the imagery as though you're painting a picture with words. Let the image inspire freeform writing, metaphors, or even poetry. Did you notice a unique quality in your writing inspired by the imagery? Write down any observations.

Want to try a yoga practice that aligns with the HeartWriting method? Head to **heartwriting.com.au** and you can join the Ten Days of HeartWriting, which includes a range of yoga classes within my ten-day beginners program.

CHAPTER EIGHT

Buddha nature in the writer

It's not easy, all this awakening and writing business. But Buddha has quite a story that ties up all this spirituality talk nicely.

Like all mythological origin stories, there's a lot of variation in the facts passed down, so I've done my best at interpreting a range of texts to create this simplified version. But as we've already learned, all texts are inherently biased, and the reader is the *real* maker of meaning.

So with that in mind, let's begin Buddha's story.

This version of the story begins around 560 B.C., when Buddha was born as a Hindu prince named Siddhārtha Gautama in Lumbini, present-day Nepal. His family ruled over the Shākya clan, meaning that Siddhārtha was raised in royalty and privilege. However, various sources claim he actually grew up in northern India, in a small, unremarkable town called Kapilavatthu – not in an opulent palace, but in a wooden house, within a strict caste system of Vedic tradition that worshipped a variety of gods and fates.

What is very true is that Siddhārtha was born into a deeply superstitious world. A group of sages visited shortly after his birth and foretold that Siddhārtha would become a holy man. His father, fearful of losing his heir, was desperate to prevent this fate. He ensured that his son's life was filled only with pleasure and protection, believing that if Siddhārtha never witnessed suffering, pain, or death, he would never seek a spiritual path. But like any curious young boy, Siddhārtha had an undeniable urge to see beyond the walls of his world.

At age 29, now married with a child, he left the palace (or home) and went into the streets. Stealthily slipping away from his parents, wife, child, and tribe, he made his escape – to find the truth and meaning of life. He finally came to witness suffering, old age, conflict and death that his father had protected him from.

The harsh journey of an ascetic

Siddhārtha set out into the vast, ancient forests surrounding the Ganges River, committing himself to an austere life as a wandering ascetic. A spiritual ascetic is a hard-core seeker of meaning – one who chooses to live apart from the world, renouncing shelter, food, and worldly possessions in pursuit of deeper truth.

On his journey, he sought out renowned teachers, learning from them in his search for life's ultimate truth and liberation. He meditated incessantly and ate very little. But in time, he realised this path was flawed. Starving the body did not awaken the mind. Enlightenment was not about removing desire, but about understanding and releasing attachment.

At the brink of death, he knew a more balanced, 'middle path' was needed.

This became known as The Middle Path – a way of wisdom, moderation, and harmony.

The awakening under the Bodhi tree

Now with a more balanced understanding, Siddhārtha sat beneath the Bodhi tree and entered deep meditation. He saw through the cycles of suffering, the illusions of the ego, and the nature of impermanence. When he opened his eyes, he was no longer Siddhārtha Gautama, the seeker. He was Buddha – the Enlightened One.

At the age of 35, Buddha gave his first teaching, known as the Four Noble Truths, which became the foundation of Buddhism. This teaching, delivered in Sarnath, India, stated:

1. That life is characterised by suffering.
2. That suffering is caused by the clinging and grasping of our own mind.
3. That it is possible to permanently end suffering.
4. The path that leads to the cessation of suffering is meditation.

Afterwards, he lifted the veil of illusion and could never return to what he once was. Now that he had seen the truth of existence, the world felt different – and a little hollow.

He grew quiet, detached, unwilling to engage in the trivial games of society.

Buddha steered clear of people-pleasing and power structures, and instead he walked the path of stillness, practiced meditation, and shared his message not through force, but through presence.

The Buddha 'Nature'

Buddha's radical insight was this: suffering is not an external punishment – it is created by the mind. He conveyed *mindfulness* as a purposeful way to dismantle our constructed reality, dissatisfactions and suffering. This was truly radical thinking at the time in a highly religious world, where the Gods were thought to hold all the power.

Liberation comes not from escaping suffering, but from facing it fully, without attachment or aversion. He said that the more we take away comforts and sit in meditation, the closer we will be to seeing truth.

Today it's easy to see his theory alive in contemporary cognitive science and its application in therapeutic settings. He established a tradition of meditation through sustained silence, philosophy, and a steadfast insistence on *mindful awareness* of the present moment.

BUDDHA'S SECRETS FOR LIFE:
reject unnecessary social norms, live in nature, open-air sleeping arrangements, once-a-day meals, frequent travel, meditation, and quietness.

The 'Buddha Nature' in the writer

Buddhism makes a lot of sense for writers. We know too well about suffering, self-doubt, rejection, and the desperate urge to cling to things that no longer serve us.

The perfection of craft takes years – and an almost super-human patience. That's why mindfulness becomes essential to our practice. Writers, like monks, sit in silence to work. We have to. While I believe that writers write best when connected to a supportive community – on the whole, writing is a pretty lonely, difficult path.

Buddha's solo journey into the darkness mirrors our own journey as writers. The forest was silent, vast, and terrifying. And your own path? It's likely tinged with doubt, uncertainty, and fear. I get it. I'm with you. And I say, congratulations. The writerly path is not an easy one, but it's worth it.

Buddha and the writer's awakening: more simple than you think

Interestingly, while Buddhist monks have practiced Kundalini and psychic-enhancing techniques for centuries, Buddha himself never taught about chakras or mystical energy centres. His teachings were simple: Detach. Meditate. See clearly. Live truthfully.

And perhaps, as writers, that's all we need to do, too. To let go of expectation, to sit in stillness and listen – not just to the world around us, but to the deeper currents within. To trust the process, even when the words don't flow. To see through illusion, through self-doubt and perfectionism, and write with clarity and courage.

Most of all, to live truthfully, knowing that every great story – like every great life – is not about chasing something outside of ourselves, but about returning home to what was within us all along. Because writing, at its core, is not just about creating stories.

It's about awakening to them.

Writing is much like Buddha's journey to enlightenment:

1. **Quest for Truth:** Just as Siddhartha embarked on a quest for truth and enlightenment, writers often embark on a quest for deeper understanding, whether it be about themselves, humanity, or the world around

them. This quest can lead writers to explore profound questions and challenge conventional beliefs.
2. **Personal Transformation:** Both new writers and the Buddha underwent significant personal transformation in their hardest times. Buddha transitioned from a life of luxury to one of asceticism and spiritual seeking, while writers undergo internal transformations of the ego as they grapple with change, social judgement, emotions, and experiences, which often find expression in their writing.
3. **Obstacles:** Buddha faced numerous challenges and obstacles on his path to enlightenment, including doubt, temptation, and the uncertainties of the unknown. Similarly, I bet you've faced obstacles such as writer's block, self-doubt, rejection, distraction, and the struggle to find your voice or message. *Me too.*
4. **Seeking Liberation:** Buddha sought liberation from suffering and the cycle of rebirth, while writers often seek liberation through their creative expression – freedom from societal constraints, freedom to explore new ideas, and freedom to share their unique perspective with the world.
5. **Impact on Others:** Just as Buddha's teachings have had a profound impact on countless individuals over the centuries, writers have the potential to influence and inspire others through their words. Whether through fiction, poetry, or non-fiction, writers have the power to evoke emotion, provoke thought, and effect change in the lives of their readers – for centuries to come. That's what I hope for you too.

PART THREE

Success

Master your craft

CHAPTER NINE

Crafting the story

'Why exactly *are* humans so wired for storytelling?' One of my Year 10 students asked me, curious and wide-eyed after I'd scribbled this line on the whiteboard, deep into teaching the foundations of fiction.

In my early days of high school teaching, I was merely a few years older than my senior students. I knew very well that I didn't have all the answers, and I was humble enough to admit it.

'That's a really good question – I'll find out more and come back to you,' I promised. It actually took me a few years to gather all the material to accurately answer this question – but at the time, all I knew for sure was: *most people love stories.* I love stories. And history tells us that stories are as ubiquitous as food and water.

My mum famously tells the story of how, at five years old, I knew the exact route to the bookstore as soon as we stepped off the bus in Perth City, and I'd trot along ahead of her, keen to immerse in a new book for the week. It was a classic story about being in love with stories.

I would get home, read all my books, then bounce my ball on the driveway and recite to myself all the tales I had just read. I would expand on them and reimagine the plotlines into epic and never-ending telenovelas in my mind.

From eight years old, every Saturday at midday I would pedal my bike as fast as I could to and from Hungry Jack's, balancing a sweaty paper bag wafting with the aroma of a large Whopper meal – then religiously set up my greasy lunch in front of the television, ready to watch an old movie – usually an Elvis classic.

I loved a good romance story. And of course, it was the suspense of the narrative structure that kept me watching. It was the fact that things went wrong, and right, and wrong, and then right again. The rollercoaster was addictive (almost as addictive as the delicious combination of beef, cheese, ketchup and pickles). I would make up my own stories in the garden afterwards, replicating the drama I'd just watched. That's when I first knew I had to be a writer, and I wanted to create stories for a living.

We are storytellers more than writers

On the road to becoming heart-led writers, it's easy to believe that our words need to constantly ooze with beauty. But the truth is, good stories represent life, which is often ugly. A story is not just a list of pretty descriptions, or a shopping list of events: it's capturing the chaos of life through the structure, art and science of narrative.

Here's the basic rule:
Bad things must happen in a story to make it a story.

Sure, good things also have to happen in a story. We can't just write about the bad things, or the good things, or there will be no story. *HeartWriters* need to be reminded that stories aren't just about butterflies and rainbows.

Thousands of years ago, Aristotle first observed that imitation, or *mimesis,* is our instinct of nature as humans. He spent much of his life studying the prevalent nature of human storytelling, and here's what he found: just like in real life, a story needs good and bad characters, action to change a situation, and a clear conclusion. Basically, we need a bunch of contrast and opposites, not 'same-same'.

And Aristotle wasn't the only one who recognised this. For millennia, humans have told compelling stories of contrast and transformation through gestures, drawings, and language (in that order). Once language fully developed, sitting around the campfire and sharing tales became a way to learn from others' experiences. Stories were not just entertainment; they were a means of survival.

A 2017 research project led by University College London's Department of Anthropology studied the Agta people, a hunter-gatherer group descended from the first people in the

> **Just like in real life, a story needs good and bad characters, action to change a situation, and a clear conclusion.**

> **Without struggle, there is no transformation; without transformation, there is no story.**

Philippines more than 35,000 years ago. The research team conducted interviews with 300 Agta individuals and found something remarkable: skilful storytelling was valued in their community more than proficiency in hunting, medicine, or any other skill. In fact, storytellers held twice as much social esteem as their most proficient hunters.

Why? Because stories weren't just told – they were tools for survival. Through storytelling, the Agta passed down essential knowledge: which plants to eat, where to find water, how to navigate conflict, how to build relationships. The stories they told were their education, their connection, their legacy.

We still use these theories today because, at its core, storytelling is the art of contrast – of light and shadow, loss and redemption, chaos and order. Without struggle, there is no transformation; without transformation, there is no story. This is why we are drawn to narrative – not just as entertainment, but as a way of making sense of our lives.

The science: it's all in the brain chemicals

So yes, humans are *wired* for storytelling as a motivation. In Joseph Campbell's classic Hero's Journey, we desperately want the character whom we are most attached to win, because we are chemically and emotionally involved. We are wired for it, just as we are wired to run from a lion or watch a traffic accident. The narrative arc taps into our evolutionary instincts, engaging our brain on a primal level.

Stories transmit information most effectively when we are given an opportunity to imagine ourselves in the story. Our brains simulate the emotions of the characters before us, creating connection; on a chemical level, the brain connection produces dopamine, which keeps us addicted to the tale. As we've already learned, we are addicts to the core: dopamine-driven beings, our brains not far evolved from our hunter-predecessors whose survival was dependent on short-term tension and reward. But it's not just dopamine that is ignited through suspenseful stories: when we get really attached to the characters, we are pumped full of oxytocin – the love drug, and we experience a phenomenon called 'transportation.' That's why we feel that the story is real, and we subsequently enter another phenomenon called 'suspension of disbelief' – a term coined by Samuel Taylor Coleridge. We cognitively know the story isn't real – but we consciously suspend that knowledge so that we can fully transport ourselves into that world. We *love it*. We want *more of it*. This wiring keeps us invested, as our brains are not only conditioned for survival but also for emotionally engaging stories that mirror the unpredictability of life.

Tragic stories are the best (for short attention spans)

Our short attention span started long before the birth of the smartphone. It was originally designed for times of threat, like when a lion was chasing us: a short burst of high focus that stimulates cortisol and a host of other chemicals. A well-crafted story creates these short bursts of tension and fear, too – often through pain and danger – just as Aristotle taught us, and just how our ancestors wired us. Our attention is likened to a spotlight, selectively focused on immediate areas of interest, and these areas of interest are hierarchical based on how dangerous they are to us physically or psychologically.

[Now, I'm willing to bet that you're nodding off already at this chapter, even though we both know that, objectively, the information discussed here is riveting for creatives! See my point? We have eased out of storytelling into an essay, and therefore ... there is no emotional engagement with characters and plot to keep our attentive brain chemicals firing. Keep going, though!]

Plot structure: Freytag's Pyramid

Freytag's Pyramid is a structural framework used to analyse and construct the narrative arc of a story, originally proposed by the 19th-century German playwright Gustav Freytag. It helps to create contrast and tension, by dividing a story into five key stages: exposition, rising action, climax, falling action, and denouement. When we divide a story into sections like this – that don't necessarily follow chronological order – we call this **plot**. *Plotting.* Organising and rearranging the story.

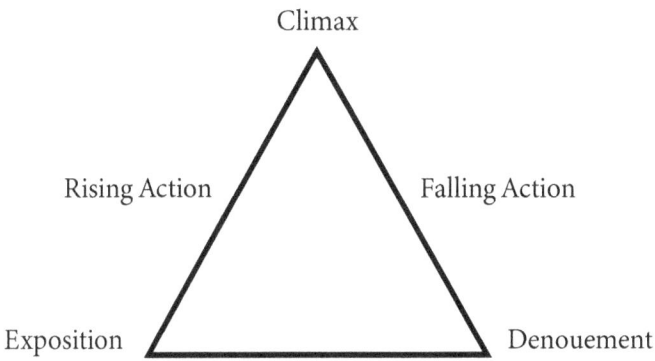

A visual representation of Freytag's Pyramid, adapted from Freytag, 1896 (Original text 1863).

- **Exposition** introduces the setting, characters, and initial conflict, establishing the foundation for the story.
- **Rising action** builds tension through a series of events and complications that lead up to the climax, where the story's central conflict reaches its peak.
- **The climax** is the turning point of the narrative, where the main character faces a decisive moment or confrontation. This rise in tension towards the climax creates chemical reactions in the listener and reader (OMG yes – please kill the bastard!) The hook is necessary to keep them invested.
- **Falling action**, following the climax, shows the consequences of the climax and leads towards resolution.

> This stage addresses the fallout from the story's peak events and begins to resolve secondary conflicts.
> - **Denouement** or **resolution** ties up loose ends and provides closure, offering a sense of completeness and stability to the narrative.

Freytag's Pyramid helps in understanding the essential components of plot development, chaos and contrast, and the emotional journey of the characters, ensuring a coherent and engaging storytelling experience.

I know plot-based stories work ...

My entire teaching career was based on the premise of storytelling. I would start the class with a personal anecdote, building tension towards a climax – and those unruly, bored students would go quiet and *lean in* to listen. You could feel the tension in the air as they anticipated the outcome of the story. Would it be laughter, or sadness?

But if I launched into theory rather than story, gazes would drop and fidgeting would start. My rebellious students would act up and create their own drama that often ended in tragedy. They inadvertently crafted real-life stories that they could then tell their friends with glee at lunchtime.

The truth is, I love personal stories just as much as my students, and I can't ignore the fact that I remember information better when it is told through the lens of a story. This is exactly why I've told many stories throughout this book.

The secret to any story's success is suspense

Suspense is the lifeblood of a great story – it keeps readers leaning in, hearts racing, waiting for the inevitable revelation. Without tension, there is no urgency, no reason to turn the page. Just as my students sat on the edge of their seats, waiting to see if my tale would end in laughter or disaster, a well-crafted story holds its audience captive.

The secret is in the build-up: yes, the slow unravelling of details, the unanswered questions, the stakes that climb higher with each beat. Whether we are writing fiction, memoir, or even explaining an idea, the plot structure of suspense – a rising arc, a pivotal climax, a satisfying resolution – is what transforms information into something memorable. Without it, a story is just noise, easily forgotten. But with it, we create something visceral, something that lingers long after the final word.

Write your story – because you have a limitless capacity for creativity inside you. In fact, it's your birthright to share your stories with the world.

PLOT BUILDING EXERCISES:

1. **The 'Plot in Reverse' Challenge:** strengthen your understanding of cause and effect within a story.

How it Works:
1. Write the climax first – a high-stake moment of conflict or revelation.
2. Then, work backward: What rising action led to this moment? What exposition set up the conditions for this event?
3. Finally, write the falling action and denouement, resolving the conflict in an unexpected but satisfying way.

Why it Works:
- Forces you to think structurally rather than just following instinct.
- Emphasises causality, helping you see how each moment builds toward the climax.
- Mimics how some great stories play with time and tension.

2. **The 'Tension Tracker' Exercise:** learn how to build suspense to engage your audience.

How it Works:
1. Choose a mundane event (e.g. making tea, waiting for a bus).
2. Rewrite the scene three times, each version increasing in tension.
   - Version 1 (Exposition & Rising Action): Describe it simply, introducing setting and characters.
   - Version 2 (Heightened Conflict): Add an unexpected complication – something is slightly off.
   - Version 3 (Climax & Fallout): Add a moment of drama or revelation that completely alters the situation.
3. Read your versions aloud (or swap with a peer) and note where tension peaks – did the reader lean in?

Why it Works:
- Helps you become aware of pacing and audience engagement.
- Reinforces the role of rising action and how small shifts in conflict keep readers invested.
- Encourages a conscious approach to tension-building, making future narratives more dynamic.

3. **'The Story Skeleton' with a Twist:** use personal storytelling to reinforce Freytag's Pyramid.

How it Works:
1. Think of a personal story that had an emotional impact – perhaps a funny, frustrating, or life-changing moment.
2. Map it onto Freytag's Pyramid, breaking it into:
   - Exposition (Where were you? What was the setup?)
   - Rising Action (What problem or tension arose?)
   - Climax (What was the pivotal moment?)
   - Falling Action (How did things start to resolve?)
   - Denouement (What was the subtle takeaway?)
3. Now, retell it dramatically – as if you were captivating a group of students in a classroom.

Why it Works:
- Reinforces how stories work instinctively in our real lives.
- Encourages oral storytelling, which strengthens narrative flow and voice.
- Shows how emotion and engagement are built naturally through structure.

CHAPTER TEN
Authentic voice

Have you ever read a book and felt like you just knew the author – like *really knew* them just by reading their words? Did you feel like their voice bounced off the page – as if you could hear them whispering or exclaiming in person? An authentic voice in writing is like hearing the tune of a great song – unmistakable, resonant, lingering in your mind, making you feel buzzed and breathless long after the last note or the final page. It's the voice that doesn't just tell a story but *breathes life into it*, making the characters, the emotions, the very world of the narrative come alive.

So what exactly is the sound of *your* writerly voice? Firstly, I'll tell you what it's not: your 'people-pleaser' voice. It took me a long time to realise this, too. It's also not created through lots of exclamation marks and BIG CAPS – in fact, the challenge is not leaning on these two things, but learning the artistry of language.

A famous example of a writer who embodies authentic voice is Elizabeth Gilbert. In *Eat, Pray, Love*, Liz writes with a voice that is as open-hearted as it is honest. She shares her journey with such warmth and vulnerability that readers feel as if they are travelling alongside her. A breath of fresh air

> **So what exactly is the sound of *your* writerly voice? Firstly, I'll tell you what it's not: your 'people-pleaser' voice.**

at the time, Gilbert's authentic voice is what made her famous. But it wasn't necessarily groundbreaking technique.

The journey to finding and honing an authentic narrative voice is both an inward and outward exploration – it is not merely about mastering techniques or adopting styles. It's more about cultivating a voice that resonates with your truth.

Carl Jung: The Voice of the Unconscious

So let's go deeper into *voice*, by diving into the subconscious – which is where truth really lies. As we discussed in previous chapters, Jung believed that our unconscious mind holds the parts of ourselves that we repress or deny – what he called the shadow. These repressed aspects can cloud our voice, causing it to sound inauthentic or forced.

To find your authentic voice, Jung suggested that we engage in the process of individuation – becoming aware of and integrating these shadow aspects into our conscious selves. This process involves recognising and accepting the darker, less comfortable parts of ourselves, which in turn allows our true voice to emerge more fully. In writing, this might mean facing the fears, doubts, or past experiences that have shaped us, and allowing these parts to inform our voice rather than suppress it. And our dreams are a big part of this work: Jung viewed dreams as direct communications from the unconscious, offering insights that our conscious minds might overlook.

Keeping a dream journal and reflecting on your nocturnal narratives can help you peel back your deeper layers, revealing a voice inside that is pumped full of truth and heart.

Opening the throat chakra to find your voice

Another step toward authentic self-expression involves opening your throat chakra (*vishuddha*), the energy centre located in the throat region, which is all about communication and truth. When this chakra is balanced, we feel empowered to speak our deepest truths without fear or self-censorship – exactly what a writer needs for a resonant, genuine voice.

Regular practices such as chanting, humming, or engaging in vocal exercises can help clear any blockages and activate this energy centre. A simple exercise a writer can use is to take a few deep breaths, then softly hum or chant the sound 'Om' (a universal vibrational sound) while focusing on the sensation in the throat. Try it now. Do you feel it? The release of energy? That sense of resonance, guidance and grounding?

You can also try singing your favourite tunes loudly in the car, or gentle neck stretches to release tension in the throat. Try freewriting directly after these vocal practices – just let the words flow without pausing to edit or judge. By combining the physical release of your throat with the creative act of writing, you'll clear a channel for your inner voice to emerge. You'll not only refine your craft – but this alignment with authentic voice empowers you to share raw, real, and powerful stories that resonate with others on a deep level, much like the heartfelt honesty we feel in writers like Liz Gilbert.

And me? How did I find my voice?

This was a cool question to ponder, because voice is my obsession, and I haven't really documented how I developed mine. So, let's see ... I'd say my most authentic voice is a combination of childhood freedom, adult experimentation, and wide reading. In a way I was really lucky that I was raised like an only child, with two big brothers who were already adults by the time I was seven. I had a lot of time and space to be as weird and whacky as I wanted to be – and these are still my favourite times in life, traipsing up and down the driveway with my magic wand or stirring potions in my garden. *I literally talked to myself,* all the time. I was deeply introverted and preferred the company of the characters in my books. I never really forgot about this side of me, and I guess I've been longing to get back there ever since. Like a deep knowing that I'm the most myself when I'm this totally eccentric kid with electrocuted hair and knobbly knees and excited eyes. I think *knowing yourself* is the key to creating an authentic voice, because then you can land on the page with integrity.

Later, in my creative writing degrees, I discovered a whole

world of late-twentieth century feminist and dystopian writing – bold, experimental stuff that completely turned my ideas upside down. I stopped watching Elvis movies and I started reading Jeanette Winterson. I was given assignments to emulate these modern and post-modern authors: to find the voice that I resonated with the most. I realised that writing is like art, and I could get away with more than I thought. I also learned that perfectionism was not the answer; I had no interest in sounding like a robot.

So yes, I had to be authentically, unashamedly me – but I also had to read and write widely in order to find my voice as a writer. But to be honest, I'm always working on voice. And it changes as I get older. I love that it's an evolution. And I love that different forms and styles of my writing will reveal a slightly different voice – some that I haven't even heard yet. A cadence or tone or phrase will appear on my page, and – *Oh. A new version of me. Hello you.*

The heart is your best compass for authenticity

So how do you really know when you've stumbled upon 'your voice'? Well, you won't know straight away, but your spiritual practices as learned in Part Two of this book will help you refine your recognition. Your true voice might sound, at first, outright weird. It might not tick all the 'good writing' boxes, and it might feel like you're blowing out all the wrong candles again. But if this is truly *you*, then don't you owe it to yourself to get to know 'you' better?

While Jung's theories provide a psychological map for finding authenticity, and the throat will help you open the door, it's the spiritual heart that acts as the most authentic compass. You might like to place a hand on your heart during meditation, and ask your heart to express its deepest truths – to bypass the ego and tap into a voice that is more aligned with your truest self. I've got plenty of meditations to help – just sing out.

Authentic voice takes time

Shaping an authentic voice in writing is a journey of its own. Some people take years of writing practice before they start to come across their most authentic written expression – but the reward of this patient practice is so brilliant, that you won't be worried about time. Your ego won't be triggered by how long this takes: with your newfound grounding as a *HeartWriter*, you'll be soothed by the sacredness of the full experience. Perhaps this is why writers tend to mature and succeed with age.

By engaging with literary techniques, exploring Jungian psychology, and connecting with the spiritual heart, you can craft a voice that is not only true to you but also resonates deeply with others. I know, with all my heart, that as you continue to write from this place of truth, your voice will naturally evolve into a unique, authentic expression that is perfectly *you*.

EXERCISES FOR FINDING YOUR AUTHENTIC VOICE

1. **Dialogue with the Self:** Begin by writing a dialogue between different parts of yourself – the conscious mind, the shadow, the heart. Let each part speak freely and without judgement. This technique, inspired by Jungian active imagination, can reveal the hidden aspects of your voice and help you integrate them into a more authentic whole. Allow the heart to have the final say, guiding the conversation toward unity and coherence.

2. **Archetypal Storytelling:** Draw on archetypal symbols and stories that resonate with your personal experiences. Consider what myths or legends have always intrigued you and why. Write a short piece that reimagines these stories through the lens of your own life. This technique not only deepens your narrative but also aligns your voice with universal themes, making it both personal and relatable.

3. **Thematic Free Writing:** Choose a theme that resonates deeply with you – love, loss, transformation – and write freely on that theme without worrying about structure or style. Focus on letting the heart guide your words, rather than the mind. This practice helps you tap into the emotional core of your voice, revealing the truths that lie beneath the surface.

4. **Voice Journalling:** Instead of a traditional journal entry, write as if you are having a conversation with a trusted mentor or a future version of yourself. Allow this voice to be unfiltered, expressing both your doubts and desires. Over time, you will notice patterns and rhythms that are unique to your voice, providing a blueprint for how you write.

5. **Heart Coherence Writing:** Engage in a heart coherence exercise before you write. Breathe deeply, focusing on your heart space, and bring to mind a moment of deep gratitude or love. Once you feel a sense of coherence, begin writing. This practice not only calms the mind but also centres your voice in the heart, ensuring that what emerges is aligned with your true self.

6. **Dream Integration:** Use your dreams as material for your writing. After recording a dream, free write about its themes and symbols, exploring how they relate to your waking life. This technique helps to integrate the unconscious elements of your psyche into your writing, lending depth and authenticity to your voice.

CHAPTER ELEVEN

Mastery

So, you want to become an award-winning creative writer? Great. You're finally overcoming your fears, you're experimenting with voice, and you understand the significance of story. Now you're ready to commit to your writing journey. But how do you start constructing your masterpiece?

It's important to recognise that sitting around, occasionally journalling, and *hoping* to become an author won't get you there. Writing is both an art and a craft, requiring dedication, structure, and the willingness to study the nuances of language.

Building your writer's toolbox

Language is a vast toolbox, and the more tools you have at your fingertips, the more powerfully you can wield your words. Each word, phrase, and sentence can be used to shape, evoke, and move. The greatest writers – whether poets, novelists, or essayists – understand that the mastery of language is essential to conveying their message with impact.

Throughout the centuries, scholars, philosophers, writers,

poets, and linguists have refined these techniques – and my goodness, I can't get enough of the smorgasbord of literary tools on offer. From Aristotle's *Rhetoric* to Virginia Woolf's stream of consciousness, the tools of language consistently nourish writers' expression in ways that resonate deeply with readers.

But so many writers don't – *or won't* – dedicate time to studying their subject. Writing, like any other craft, requires deliberate practice. Even if, like me, you believe that much of your writing is inspired by spirit, you are empowered to express those spiritual insights more effectively when you can channel them through language techniques that have proven their impact across time. After all, your audience is human, and the way humans connect with words has been studied, explored, and understood for generations.

You need to learn and refine your skills continuously, much like a sculptor patiently chisels away at marble to reveal the form within. Me? I'm still learning! It's a lifelong commitment to become a writer, so keep studying. Here's four of my favourite tools that you can add to your writer's toolbox – but I teach many more in my signature course.

Tool 1: Reading

Immersing yourself in the works of others is like being an apprentice with the masters of the craft. But it's astonishing how many aspiring writers overlook the importance of reading – and I know this, because so many people come to me wanting to learn to write, but admit that they read very little. Or – they simply read the same types of books over and over again. But nothing is challenged or expanded by staying put in your comfort zone. Reading widely and deeply exposes you to different styles, voices, and techniques, helping you to discern what works and what doesn't – for you, at least. Sure, you won't enjoy every new book, but you will absorb new rhythms, structures, and stylistic choices from this wide range of authors, even without consciously analysing them. Over time, this exposure sharpens your own writing, allowing you to experiment to find what works best for you.

I'm no different to you – without all the books I was forced to read in high school English Literature, and then my three subsequent degrees, I would not have stumbled upon authors that have shaped my very own unique style: a style that might not be fully showcased in this book, but you'll witness widely in my fiction writing.

Let me tell you about my love affair with Tim Winton. I first read his books in high school in Western Australia – of course, a freshly famous WA author was high up on the curriculum. By the time I got to studying *Cloudstreet* in English Literature in Year 12, I was well and truly in love. This book probably shaped me as a person and a writer more than any other book in my life. It also helped that I had to read it four times in a short space of time, and I spent the entire year analysing – with the help of my teacher – all its literary devices in fine detail.

I loved that Winton broke many rules. This made me realise what I wanted to do with my fiction. I wanted to be different. More than anything, I wanted to create emotion. His flavourful characterisation and poetic technique – in particular, his unique syntax – created an energy and emotion in me which kept me deeply in love with characters like Dolly and Fish until this very day.

But for a number of years – when I was high school teaching – I stopped reading books *for me* because I was so focused on student curriculum. It's no wonder that my creativity dried up. It wasn't until I started my postgraduate studies that I was introduced to a pile of brand-new writers. Some of these writers leaped drastically out of Winton's world of modernism into the chaotic throes of postmodernism – challenging my expectations to such a degree that I found it difficult to read these texts. But under the right teachers I learned just how powerful these writers could be. I dove into Bernardine Evaristo's postmodern novel titled *Girl, Woman, Other* and saw more meaning on the page than I had seen in years – a book filled with experimental voice and structure, with literally no full stops until the end of each chapter. *Ah, another rule I could break!* And then I read Evaristo's memoir, penned in her much more 'normal' prose style, which probably sounded more like her real voice, and I came to realise that inside even the most 'extra' of authors is just a normal human being – like me. That means, *I can do this too*. Each book I devoured gave me new ideas, and new hope that I could make it.

Each writer and each story is a unique expression, offering lessons in what makes writing effective. What leaves a lasting impact on you, and why? What makes a Booker Prize winner stand out from the crowd? Can you deconstruct its magic, identifying the techniques that make it powerful? Notice how the voice of the narrator or characters is crafted. What makes this voice distinct? What elements of the writing make it revealing, moving, or profound? Dissect the descriptions – what do they convey beyond the surface? Consider the actions depicted in the story – how do they resonate emotionally or intellectually?

By analysing these aspects, you begin to see the machinery behind the narrative, the gears that make the story tick. And, most importantly, can you experiment with these techniques in your own work, adapting them to fit your voice and vision?

Tool 2: Symbolism using the metaphor (not the cliché)

Metaphors are both overrated and underrated. It's all how you use them – and how often.

A metaphor describes one thing as something else, symbolically, with the aim of creating a visual or sensory comparison. Metaphors are the symbolic phrases in writing: when we represent something with something else to amplify the meaning, feeling, or image. For example, if we compare the fluffy clouds to white marshmallows, there's no need to use excess adjectives to describe the clouds – the marshmallow image does it all for you. It also creates a warm, sweet feeling, as marshmallows are associated with happy family times, enjoying a sweet, soft delight immersed in a chocolatey drink – comfort, love, warmth.

> 'The clouds are pink marshmallows
> against the setting sun'

A simile does the same thing, but uses *like*, *than* or *as* to make the comparison.

> 'The clouds are *like* pink marshmallows'
> 'The clouds are *as* fluffy *as* marshmallows'
> 'The clouds are fluffier *than* marshmallows'

It's important to use metaphors to increase the vibrancy and meaning of the image, but beware of the poet who uses too many of them. Also beware of clichés: metaphors that have been used too often and have lost their meaning and effect. Or the worst of all: mixed metaphors! Before you know it, the plane of love that's flying away has suddenly become a monster-ship? Be careful!

Tool 3: Sound techniques: alliteration and onomatopoeia

> The *b*ees *b*uzzed around the *b*ountiful garden.

I'm a big fan of alliteration: the repetition of consonant sounds at the beginning of closely positioned words. It's a powerful stylistic device in creative writing – but we must remember to use it with care and moderation. It enhances the rhythm, mood, and memorability of a passage, often imbuing the text with a musical quality – but if overused, or poorly used, it will have the opposite effect.

This technique can be used to draw attention to specific phrases, create a sense of unity, or emphasise themes. A great example of effective alliteration comes from Booker Prize-winning novel *The God of Small Things* by Arundhati Roy, where alliteration is used to create a poetic rhythm and to highlight the lush, evocative nature in her prose:[4]

> '*Esthappen and Rahel woke to the <u>sh</u>out of*
> *<u>s</u>leep <u>s</u>urprised by <u>sh</u>attered kneecaps.*'

In this sentence, the repetition of the 's' sound in 'shout,' 'sleep,' 'surprised,' and 'shattered' creates a hissing sound effect, known as sibilance, which enhances the intensity of the scene.

Another example of effective alliteration is found in *Lincoln in the Bardo* by George Saunders, a postmodern literary book that explores identity and reality:[5]

> '<u>B</u>ut soon, I think? she said.
> *Her <u>b</u>eauty swelled <u>b</u>eyond description.*
> *And I <u>b</u>urst into tears.*'

True to the postmodern era, Saunders uses satire through the deliberate *overuse* of alliteration. The repetition of the 'b' sound in 'beauty' 'beyond,' and 'burst' creates a swelling and breathless rhythm that mirrors the overwhelming emotions of the narrator. It symbolises a moment of realisation or transition, much like how the novel explores metaphysical shifts and the afterlife.

My other favourite sound technique is onomatopoeia: words that sound like what they mean. Buzz, pop, bang, crack ... Can you think of ten more words?

Tool 4: Diction and syntax: mastery of words in sentences

Use the right word – not two words, not ten words. Just one perfect word.

Diction, or word choice, is an important element in creative writing because it directly influences the tone, style, and meaning of a story. The specific words an author selects will evoke emotion, set the mood, and establish voice. For instance, using vivid, descriptive language can create a wondrous and wild scene, while harsh or restrained diction can convey coldness or mystery.

Her hands soared in the direction of the outheld ice-cream.

Through the carefully chosen word 'soared' we register a sense of freedom and ecstasy in the character. She feels childlike, hopeful and authentic, to me.

Now, think about yourself as a character. What would you want readers to know or feel about you? How about the words you use in dialogue – what could they convey? The way you speak and the specific words you use can reflect your socio-economic status, education, personality, preferences, and experiences. This attention to language helps create distinct, believable voices in narratives.

The specific words an author selects will evoke emotion, set the mood, and establish voice.

Diction can also help us shape place and context. *The Great Gatsby* uses highly evocative and precise language to paint the opulence and decay of the Jazz Age.[6] For instance, in describing Gatsby's parties, Fitzgerald writes:

> *'In his blue gardens men and girls came and went like moths among the whisperings and the champagne and the stars.'*

Here, Fitzgerald's choice of words – 'blue gardens,' 'moths,' 'whisperings,' and 'champagne' – not only creates a lush, sensory-rich image of Gatsby's world, but also conveys the superficiality of the 1920s social scene. (Fitzgerald himself famously coined the term 'Jazz Age' to describe the spirit and excesses of the United States following World War I.)

Not only does his diction enhance the sense of glamour and emptiness, but the long winding sentences with repetitions of 'and' to connect numerous items and comparisons, reflects the novel's themes of high decadence and disillusionment. This technique is called *syntax*.

Syntax is about sentence creation. It involves arranging

words to create logical phrases and sentences. The word syntax stems from the Greek *syntassein*, which contains the preface syn- meaning 'together' and tassein 'arrange'. It also comes from the French *syntaxe*, which means the 'systematic arrangement of parts'. Syntax differs from diction (word choice) because it's more about the unique placement of words together.

But not everything has to be grammatically correct. When it comes to syntax, it's more important to create flow and feeling across the sentence. Short sharp, and even incomplete sentences create a grating, cold effect. Long, luminous, winding sentences with lots of 'ands' (conjunctions) creates a whimsical, glorious feeling. And the way you play around and arrange these sentences – and paragraphs – can change everything.

Lastly: Language evolves, so chill out about the rules

As you delve deeper into your craft, you'll soon realise that there is no single 'right' way to write. Language is fluid and constantly evolving – like fashion. What resonates in one era may shift in another (and sometimes comes back in fashion like the flared jeans I so love – ha!) The key is to find what feels right for you. Experiment, take risks, and forge your own path through the literary landscape to find out what kind of writer you are.

But this creative freedom comes with a caveat: to innovate, you should understand the foundations first. Get yourself acquainted with the great canon of literature. Discover and learn the breadth of techniques – otherwise, how will you know what's worked and what hasn't, and for whom, and why? You need something to compare yourself to, and something to build upon. *So get building those foundations.*

EXERCISES TO REFINE YOUR CRAFT

Here are three fun writing exercises designed to help you analyse, experiment with, and refine your writing craft.

1. **The Booker Prize Breakdown**
    1. Choose an award-winning novel (e.g. a Booker Prize winner) or a book you deeply admire.
    2. Analyse its magic:
        - Voice: How is the narrator or character's voice crafted? What makes it unique?
        - What sound and visual techniques evoke strong emotions in the reader?
        - How do descriptions go beyond the surface – what is suggested rather than stated?
    3. Rewrite a passage in your own voice: Take a short excerpt and rewrite it as if you had written it, keeping the same tone, emotion, and impact, but adjusting it to fit your style.
    4. Reflect: What changed? What stayed the same? How did experimenting with another writer's technique influence your own?

2. **The Genre Swap Experiment**
    1. Take a paragraph from a novel you admire (or one of your own pieces).
    2. Rewrite it in a different genre or style:

- If it's literary fiction, turn it into noir.
- If it's a mystery, rewrite it as a poetic reflection.
- If it's historical fiction, make it sci-fi.
3. Pay attention to voice, sentence rhythm, and mood.
4. Reflect: How does genre shape language and emotional resonance?

3. **The Voice Experiment: Borrow, Break, and Build**
   1. Borrow: Select a passage from a writer with a strong, unmistakable voice (e.g. Arundhati Roy, Zadie Smith, Tim Winton). Write a paragraph mimicking their style – adopt their rhythm, sentence structure, and tone.
   2. Break: Rewrite the paragraph, breaking one major stylistic element – perhaps making it more concise, adding poetic devices like alliteration, or changing the perspective.
   3. Build: Finally, rewrite the paragraph in your own voice while maintaining the emotional weight of the original.

Reflection: What stylistic elements did you keep? What felt unnatural or forced? How did this exercise help you refine your unique storytelling voice?

CHAPTER TWELVE
Community

A year before I embarked upon my solo travels, I booked myself on a Contiki tour and, surrounded by 50 other young people, including my friend Lenny, I discovered the world for the first time – and what a discovery I made. It was not just the landscapes that made a huge impression on me, but the *people* I was sharing this experience with. We're human, after all, and we are deeply motivated by relationship. I learned so much about the world on those sunrise debriefs on the morning coach – or the late-night conversations over wine – or laughing over forkfuls of garlic-fried snails in Paris.

One afternoon I wandered the Parisian streets alone. I felt my heart fill with joy as I walked the cobblestone banks of the River Seine, taken by rectangles of ubiquitous artwork perched on all corners, from classical watercolours to crazy slashes of funky art. *Paris has no rules!* – I thought to myself, comparing to my world back home. People dressed and spoke with personality and vibrancy. And in the background of the wash of people and art, I saw coloured lights and umbrellas against the prettiness of the silver-set water. Couples kissed unashamedly on the banks. People padlocked their love to the bridges.

'Padlock *me* to that bridge! I am totally in love with this place,' I said to Lenny that night as we dined together, comparing what we'd seen on the streets that day. He shared with me his photos and insights from his own solo day out, and together, we formed a deeper understanding of French culture. Across the table, every single Contiki member we'd been sharing the bus with shouted stories at each other in a drunken garble, all teaching a new way of seeing the world. And what a magnificent world it was.

We become something so much more when we share knowledge with others. Just like our predecessors who shared tales over campfires tens of thousands of years ago, we are always a better, rounder, more *skilled version of self* when we join hands with community.

And there is no exception when it comes to being a writer.

The myth of the isolated writer

The romantic image of the isolated writer toiling away in solitude is a total myth – because in reality, good writers don't work alone. Think of your favourite author. They have a team behind them making sure their work is brushed clean of any errors – and that's just the tip of the iceberg. Imagine how many friends, mentors, editors, agents, and writing communities they have worked with to bring their words and ideas to life.

Writers draw perspective, inspiration, and critical feedback from their communities. They need other writers, mentors, and friends who understand the realities of the creative process. Writing, like any other craft, thrives in an environment rich with support, shared learning, and collaboration.

The loneliness of the writing life: a breeding ground for fear

Look, I'm not saying that writers don't spend a significant time alone to get the job done. Yes, writing *is* inherently lonely work. Unlike painters who might create their art in public or musicians who perform live to the applause of an audience, writers often work in large chunks of silence. Their craft unfolds in private at a desk, or perhaps perched in front of a picturesque beach, but almost always averted from the immediate gaze of others. And it does need to be this way – otherwise your glorious words don't get written. There's something to be said for the space and silence of the creative alpha brainwave, and this dreamy way of being requires you to steer clear of the fast-paced conversation that resides in the home of the beta brainwave. But this necessary isolation can lead to a pervasive feeling of invisibility that can breed self-doubt and fear.

When I worked as a magazine editor, I experienced this loneliness firsthand. The office, though filled with other writers and editors, was often silent. Each person was absorbed in their work, crafting articles alone at their desks. While at first I loved this newfound quiet – such a calm change from the noisy high school environments I had worked in before! – I couldn't fight the feeling of isolation that came with it. Soon enough, I made friends with the other editors, and then the gifts of creative collaboration kept coming my way.

The solution isn't to resign yourself to a life of feeling alone – it's to seek out pockets of time with community. (And I mean the right community: the community that provides you insight and inspiration, not those who ply you with wine, cheese and gossip and let you roll home without a single brain cell left). Writers need insight, encouragement, and constructive criticism that comes from being part of a community of like-minded people. And gosh, am I grateful for my fellow editors – who are still my best friends. I'm always bouncing ideas off them. I live for literary conversations. I love asking them if the comma goes here, there, or not at all.

Conscious creative community

A writing community is not just a place for praise. Please don't join writer's groups just to seek approval – this is leading you back to that dangerous ego territory back in Chapter Three. Rather, a shared writing space is where writers can hone their craft – with support. In a workshop or writing group, the playing field is levelled: everyone is there to improve, to share their work, and to give and receive constructive feedback. The magic of these groups lies in their ability to foster growth, not through competition, but through collaboration and mutual respect.

Recognising that you and your fellow writers are all in it to hone your craft allows you to see each other as allies rather than competitors. Yes! We find the *heart* in conscious creative community. In these spaces, the goal is not to win praise but to learn, to experiment, and to refine your voice. That's why writing groups can provide the encouragement and accountability that solitary writing often lacks. By sharing your work with others, you invite new perspectives and insights that can illuminate aspects of your writing you may not have seen on your own – just as my insights about Paris were so strengthened when I shared them with Lenny.

Learning from literary friends and mentors

In Australia, the friendship between Helen Garner and Tim Winton is a testament to the power of creative connection. Both writers, celebrated for their evocative prose (with very different styles) have supported and influenced each other over the years. Their friendship shows us that even the most solitary of crafts can benefit from the exchange of ideas and the sharing of struggles.

Winton's work, deeply rooted in small town Australian landscape, was not an immaculate conception. Winton was taught by the great Elizabeth Jolley at Curtin University, forming the backbones of his breakthrough fame with his first book, *An Open Swimmer*.

A few years after first studying Winton's work, I found myself in the Elizabeth Jolley Theatre at Curtin, guided by lecturers who had once been taught by Jolley herself. Twelve years after that, on the other side of Australia, I was mentored by a range of authors in my master's – some of whom had crossed paths with both Helen Garner and Tim Winton.

Writers like Winton would not have found their signature style without mentors. Nor would I have found mine. Learning is a beautiful thing, and it's not just for a limited few. It's for us all. If you think you've got nothing to learn about writing, think again.

Literary friendships are not just about social connection – they are about creating a space where learning can flourish. In these spaces, writers find the courage to explore and refine their craft, and the support to persevere through the inevitable challenges of the writing life.

Criticism and feedback is a loving gesture

In the *HeartWriting* community, surrounded by fellow writers who share your passion for literature *and heart*, you are supported in your quest to develop an authentic voice, one that resonates with both your inner truth and the readers you seek to reach.

This allows you to embrace criticism wholeheartedly – which is essential for growth. The best writers are often those who are equally loved and criticised – a polarity that indicates that your work touches the hearts of a specific audience rather than attempting to please everyone. So get resilient with the help of your peers – because nobody can please everyone!

Criticism, when offered thoughtfully and received with an open heart, can be a powerful tool for improving your writing craft. It's easy to fall into the trap of people-pleasing, of wanting to write something that everyone will love. But true artistry comes from taking risks, from being willing to create work that might polarise your audience. To grow as a writer, you must be willing to walk into the unknown, to push the boundaries of your comfort zone, and to accept that not everyone will appreciate your work.

The more feedback you receive, the more opportunities you have to grow. But it's essential that this feedback comes from the right people. Feedback from your best friend or cousin – someone who is not familiar with the nuances of writing – might be well-intentioned but totally unhelpful. This is why being part of an aligned writing group is so essential, because you'll gain insights from people who know what they're talking about, and will ultimately help you improve.

Start or join a writing group

If you're serious about developing your craft, consider starting or joining a writing group. *HeartWriting* is built on the philosophy that writing is a communal activity, enriched by the feedback and support of others. In these groups, you'll learn how to give and receive feedback without fear, guided by the loving powers of your heart. It's a beautiful way to create, connect, and grow as a writer, ensuring that your journey is one of continuous learning and heartfelt communication.

Being part of a writing community also provides accountability. When you know that others are expecting to read your work and offer feedback, you're more likely to stay committed to your writing practice. This sense of responsibility can be a powerful motivator, helping you to push through moments of doubt or writer's block.

So, what are you waiting for?

The following activities on '*community*' are from the *Ten Days of HeartWriting* course. Enjoy!

COMMUNITY EXERCISE 1:

Write and send a letter to a loved one

- Use your blossoming writing skills to connect with someone you love. Write them a heartfelt letter, just like the 'old days', in long form. Firstly, explain to your new pen pal that this is a *HeartWriting* activity, and you would be keen to start up a monthly letter swap with them to keep up the momentum of heartfelt writing.

- In your letter, share with them your life journey lately. Go into particular detail on one scene in your life – perhaps when you walked in nature, learned to meditate, or experienced the joys of poetry.

- Make sure you include some well-placed, original metaphors in your letter – but not too many. *Like Goldilocks ... justttt right.*

- Don't just email the letter ... send it in the post! That will ensure the ultimate surprise, and will deepen your heartfelt pen pal connection.

COMMUNITY EXERCISE 2:

Have you ever wondered how writers stay connected?

Your task today is to research some famous writers from the 19th and 20th centuries (you'll find the most documentation on those two centuries), and find out what kind of studies they undertook, and who they hung out with – i.e. the writing friends and networks they nurtured. You might like to search the following famous writers: Jack Kerouac, Toni Morrison, Margaret Atwood, Ernest Hemingway, Charles Dickens, Mary Shelley, Truman Capote, John Keats, Judy Blume, Harper Lee, Zadie Smith.

CHAPTER THIRTEEN
Devotion to completion

Creative practice is more than just self-expression; it's a form of devotion to life. When we commit to our creative practice, we're making a promise to honour our true selves, to listen to the whispers of our hearts, and to give voice to the truths that reside within us. Our work becomes a sacred offering to the world.

Devotion to our craft requires discipline, patience, and a willingness to be vulnerable. It means showing up for our creative work even when it feels difficult, even when doubt and fear threaten to silence our voices. By dedicating time and energy to our creative practice, we realise our worth. Our stories, art, and contributions to the world matter – and we commit to completing them, rather than letting all our creative ideas float into the ether.

Julia Cameron, author of *The Artist's Way,* describes how creativity is a spiritual practice. It is not something we do; it is something we become. This shift from doing to *being* switches us into the ultimate gear of creative reverence and devotion – because when we view our creativity as an integral part of *who* we are, we begin to treat it with the respect and care it deserves.

But writing is a challenging, time-consuming vocation. It's easy to give up – or let life take over. If you're not careful, years will pass and a project will gather dust. When your motivation wavers, my best advice is to head back to nature. Find what leaves you in awe. Let that be your prayer.

> **When your motivation wavers, my best advice is to head back to nature. Find what leaves you in awe. Let that be your prayer.**

Nature is our temple of creative devotion

As I learned during all my adventures – and now, at home in my beachside treehouse – nature is the ultimate temple to reignite your creative motivation. Maybe your fight to finish your project is wavering. Maybe you've lost the words for a few weeks. But when you lean into nature, you are reminded of the source of all life.

Let's begin by walking to the closest tree you can find. Now look at the leaves. Are they forest green, or emerald, or – ? Take a leaf and roll it between your fingertips, taking note of the texture. How about the smell? Is there an interesting sound as the leaves flutter high above you? A metaphor that you can use to describe it? Finding your way back to nature is the perfect route to return to your writing, because it is all about aliveness in experience *and* description.

Nature also reminds us of the cycles of life. Everything starts; everything ends. Just as your project starts – one day it must end. As a writer, you need to trust in these cycles – and complete them. Mother Earth shows up in mythology as the ultimate creatrix goddess, the one who nurtures and sustains all life. Gaia, the Greek primordial Earth goddess, and Danu, the Celtic mother goddess, represent the Earth's fertility, abundance, and creative power – qualities that are mirrored in the act of writing. Ebb and flow, growth and decay, light and shadow, the constant shift of the seasons. Everything is connected somehow, from birth, to the return to the earth. Just like the Earth goes through its cycles of life and regeneration, so do our works of art. Knowing this inspires us to keep going, because we're not just working by ourselves – we're in cahoots with the universe.

From devotion to completion

Writing is a sacred birth. It's a writer's way of giving back to the mysteries of creation. Think of yourself as a literary shaman, venturing into the heart of the universe and returning with stories that heal, inspire, and delight. Keeping this in mind reminds you *why* you began writing in the first place. Every time you feel stuck, let that bigger purpose guide you back to your desk (or your favourite sunny patch of grass) and ignite your determination to see it through.

Treat your craft like it's sacred: as though your writing is your dharma, your divine purpose. Devote yourself to it. And yes, *finish* it. Let the momentum of that cosmic connection carry you all the way to 'The End,' knowing that completing your project isn't just a personal triumph ... it's your gift to the great dance of creation we're all part of.

The Sustainable Creative Garden

I decided long ago that I didn't want to be one of those writers who burn out before they get started. I wanted to be in it for the long haul, and that meant doing it right: by cultivating a life of creativity and resilience. I developed a system I call my Sustainable Creative Garden, which helps me stay focused and productive, even when times get tough.

Here's how it works:

Tending: Make space in your life for creativity to grow organically. This means setting aside time and mental space for your creative pursuits.

Weeding: Remove distractions that drain your emotional and physical energy, allowing you to focus more fully on your creativity.

Seeding: Write daily. Create daily. Not too little, not too much. Water your creative garden regularly, but don't drown it.

Cultivating: Join groups, classes, and workshops to meet others and learn. A supportive community will help cultivate your creativity.

Harvesting: Enjoy the fruits of your creative labours. Celebrate your successes and share your work with the world.

Keep Going: Continue to nurture your creative garden, and each year, your crop will grow more abundant and prosperous. You've got this!

The world needs your story

It's important that you complete your story, no matter how long it takes – because the world needs it. Today, stories are more important than ever. When we witness the profound impact of David Attenborough's *Life on Planet Earth* or Tim Winton's *Ningaloo Nyinggulu*, we see firsthand how stories can inspire change. These documentaries are not just visual masterpieces; they are cleverly curated narratives – *yes, stories!* – that evoke emotion and move us to action. We talk about these stories, these films, for weeks, months, and even years, just like every other story that has touched us deeply. And guess what: these films began as *written* words, carefully crafted by a team of writers before they were taken to the screen.

As writers, our task is no less vital today than it was in Aristotle's time. Writing is not a luxury; it's a vital tool for humanity. We still use it every day. And stories are more important now than ever. While it may not be as immediately necessary as carpentry to keep a roof over our heads, writing inspires and helps us understand the world. Without it, we would miss out on one of the most important aspects of being human – the ability to connect through stories.

This is more than just you

Yes, your writing is more than just about you! Completing a significant writing project is no small feat, especially when you're writing from the heart – and driven by a bigger mission. As a *HeartWriter*, your work isn't just about putting words on paper; it's about creating something that resonates deeply with your inner truth and has the power to touch and transform others. I *know* the journey to finishing a big project can be daunting, but with strategy and heart, it can also be the most rewarding task of your life.

Take time to reflect on the larger purpose behind your project. Ask yourself: What message am I/ is spirit trying to convey? How can this work serve others? Reaffirming your mission can reignite your passion and give you the energy to push through your low moments. You can do this! Just keep reflecting – and showing up to your desk.

How to finish the project

1. Reconnect with your why
When you're in the thick of a large writing project, it's easy to lose sight of why you started in the first place. The daily grind of writing, editing, and revising – *ugh* – can sometimes

overshadow the passion that initially prompted your work. Regularly reconnect with your mission – you know, the reason why you chose to embark on this journey in the first place.

2. Break it down into manageable steps

A big writing project can feel overwhelming when viewed as a whole. To maintain momentum, break the project down into smaller, more manageable steps. Create a plan with specific milestones and deadlines. This approach not only makes the work more approachable but also gives you a sense of progress as you complete each step. I have some planning templates for you – head to **heartwriting.com.au/thehandbook** to find your bonus resources!

3. Get an editor

Hiring an editor is invaluable for any writer, whether you're a seasoned author or just starting out. All those books you see on the bookshelves in the shops? They all were refined by numerous editors. Not one – several! I hope that feels humbling for you – you should not have to do this alone. An editor or book mentor brings a fresh, objective perspective to your work, while ironing out any issues, refining your ideas, and polishing your prose to ensure that your message is clear and impactful. A good editor will catch errors and inconsistencies you might not see, offer insights on structure and flow, and provide guidance on how to strengthen your narrative or argument: making it the best possible work it can be. Remember, this book was professionally edited, too!

4. Seek support from your creative community

Finishing a big project is easier when you have a supportive network to lean on. Surround yourself with fellow writers, mentors, and friends who understand your journey and can offer encouragement, feedback, and accountability. Share your progress with them and don't hesitate to ask for help when needed. Plus, knowing that others are going through the same thing – and that they believe in your mission – can be a powerful motivator to keep going.

5. Embrace the imperfections

Perfectionism is one of the biggest obstacles to finishing a writing project. The desire to make every word perfect can lead to endless revisions and a fear of letting go. As a *HeartWriter*, it's important to remember that your work doesn't have to be flawless to be meaningful. The imperfections in your writing are often what make it authentic and relatable.

6. Celebrate each milestone

Celebrate each milestone you reach, no matter how small. These celebrations can be simple – like taking a walk in nature, enjoying a favourite treat, or clinking a cocktail with loved ones. Acknowledging your progress reinforces your commitment and keeps your spirits high as you move toward the finish line. Allow yourself to let go of the need for perfection and focus instead on the positive impact your words will have on others.

As you approach the end of your project, remember that finishing strong is about staying true to your heart and your mission. It's about honouring the creative journey and recognising the value of what you've put out to the world. There – you've fulfilled your calling.

Wow, you've finished your big writing project!

The act of completing something you've poured your heart into brings a sense of closure, peace, and *santosha,* the Sanskrit word for deep contentment. This process has not just been about producing something – it has also been a practice of *honouring your sacred heart* while learning more about your craft, your voice, and your unique creative offering. And now that you're finished, it's time to show the world – and it's time to create more glorious things from the heart.

The impact of your words will extend way beyond the page. It will touch lives, inspire change, and create deep healing. *Can you feel that?* Yes, soon your work will become part of a larger conversation, adding to the richness of human expression and experience: a contribution that is a true gift to the world, one that can have ripple effects for years to come.

Don't worry yourself right now with questions and concerns like 'How will I publish?' or 'Maybe nobody will want to read my book.' I had all the same worries too – we all do. But somehow all the answers unravel in good time. Just finish your book with confidence and heart. During inevitable moments of struggle, look into book mentoring (I host an online book writing program for heart-led writers). Hire an editor – the important next step after completion to shape and refine your work. In the meantime, re-read Part Two of this book. Keep your heart open. And remember that *slow and steady wins the race* – it's all in divine timing.

To truly succeed beyond the creation and completion of a book, we must choose ourselves. We must choose to love each cell, each beat, each whisper of our hearts. We must choose to expand that love to the world around us. We must choose to use words that speak from the heart. We must choose to make positive, lasting change, even when our stories hurt to write. Your words can truly change the world, but only if you commit to putting them on paper.

Every day, I sit, I write, and I work at it gently and lovingly. I tune in to the sound of my heart, listening with every cell, with every fibre of my being. Writing has become an act of pure love for me since I made a pact to let go of all my distractions and dramas – and instead I devote to the act of writing as meditation, grace, dharma.

This love fuels my writing, keeping the fire alive, making it a practice that keeps me creating – no matter what.

Now, when I fully embrace my heart, I become a powerful truth-telling writer, full of life and voice. I am me. I am unique. Sure, I am often weird. I am not always perfect. But still I honour myself. I honour all writers. I honour each unique voice. I love all beings on this planet. It starts with me, and this love expands outwards. I love everything and everyone, unconditionally. This love fuels my writing, keeping the fire alive, making it a practice that keeps me creating – no matter what.

A final note to the struggling artist:

When the heart hurts, please seek help

Growing up in a family affected by mental health issues and suicide, I've seen firsthand the importance of addressing these struggles, especially as a writer. It's all too common to hear about the 'tortured artist' who writes from a place of trauma without seeking help to return to the light. Some writers become addicted to their pain, but I believe it's crucial to take mental health seriously. In my experience, mental health issues often start with broken connections and closed hearts – both of which can be healed, and both of which benefit immensely from creative acts as a form of healing.

Many people with broken hearts or overwhelmed minds hesitate to seek help due to fear, shame, unworthiness, finances, or simply apathy that spirals into major depression. Yet, those who hesitate often have the privilege and resources to find help. Even if financial barriers exist, there are local and global organisations, government healthcare, and charities that won't turn you away from getting the help you need to stay healthy and alive.

The other alarming default that is on the rise is destructive anger – understandably fuelled by raging wars, political turmoil, and climate crises, rendering us furious at the world and in turn shutting down hearts and creative solutions.

Anger is not a bad thing in and of itself. It is a powerful human emotion necessary to shift trapped trauma, or create waves of change. But, left to fester *en masse*, it's an emotion that will lead humanity down a dark path if we don't channel it somewhere more heart-centred and solution-oriented.

Don't deflect your privilege by choosing a life of anger, martyrdom or victimhood. You won't save the world by thinking this way. Instead, you can help the world by taking the opportunities in front of you – getting the mental health support you need, and building compassion and *resilience*, so that you can be of help, not hindrance. When you're stronger, you can assist others in need. You can write about your experiences, design volunteer projects, or organise charity events. The world needs *more people like you* to raise the collective vibration and open more hearts if we hope to see a better, more compassionate world emerge.

If you're struggling to find solutions, start by closing your eyes and asking the universe for guidance. Tune in to one of my meditations on the *HeartWriting* podcast. Often, we just need to take the time to connect with our hearts.

CHAPTER FOURTEEN
Full circle

I'm a writer, and I've come full circle.

I'll be totally honest with you. Despite this book of creative inspiration, if I had unlimited funds I would never have come back from my travels. I'm not just an emotional addict and a praise addict – I'm also a *travel* addict. There's nothing quite like the dopamine rush of waking up in a new city. The ultimate blank page. *I don't have to be anyone at all here. I'm free.*

At the time, I was so far from reality and I was so 'living the dream', I couldn't believe I hadn't done it earlier in life. But everything happens for a reason. Suddenly the funds dried up, and travelling for travel's sake wasn't hitting the spot. Eventually my heart and my bank balance brought me back to Australia to regroup. Perhaps it was simply divine destiny – I was meant to come home to make a better plan. *What exactly did I want from life?*

> **Despite what I thought I wanted – fun, freedom, fantasy – the universe pivoted my path anyway, back to my heart's desire.**

Despite what I thought I wanted – fun, freedom, fantasy – the universe pivoted my path anyway, back to my heart's desire. It didn't have to be a conscious wake-up call. *What was meant to be was meant to be.* Just like how this book has ended up in your hands. What will you do with the energy and information shared in these fourteen chapters?

What happened next was all relatively effortless and unconscious.

Because I was out of money, I moved back in with my old housemate in Perth and went back to a full-time teaching job to recoup my funds. I was depressed and started experiencing chronic migraines and panic attacks for the first time in my life. The body doesn't lie. My whole being was subconsciously telling me to take action. This forced me to seek out doctors, psychologists and healers. I threw all my money and time into getting better. At some stage I heard my heart speak to me with some clear words of direction, as I told you about in Chapter Five: 'You are going to be a professional writer. You'll travel far to become this writer. You'll ...' I kept these words on conscious repeat as I fumbled through work, healing, heartbreak.

One psychologist created a big fancy diagram on a miniature whiteboard. 'This is the circle of life,' she said slowly and irritatingly through perfectly painted red lips. 'When you merge this circle with this circle and this circle, here, in the middle, is where you find happiness.'

I didn't know what the hell she was on about because my mind was so rattled. All I knew was my job was not providing me happiness – nor was getting drunk and dating the wrong men. I felt, deep in my bones, that I needed a new start. But I couldn't just pack up and travel this time. I had to do something about the monster inside me.

I went home and scrolled socials. Then I Googled: **Creative Writing Master's Degrees in Sydney and Melbourne.** I kept circling back to two links: RMIT, or UTS? *Melbourne, or Sydney?*

Sydney won. My decision had something to do with more calendar days of sunshine.

The return of Jack

'Oh my god ... Jack – he lives in Sydney!' I thought to myself after I'd booked the ticket and applied – with success – for the master's program. *A friend! A friend in Sydney!* I texted him: 'Hey, I'm moving to Sydney! Let's catch up!'

I arrived in Sydney with two suitcases and a giant backpack: 52 kg of luggage (the weight of my luggage was more than the weight of my skinny-ass depressed body). I took a selfie with all my suitcases and bags in the airport lift. I remember the moment. I still have the photo. I was simultaneously shaking and *really fucking thrilled*. I closed my eyes, soothed by a vision of a sacred circle of writers sitting in nature, the same vision I'd had months earlier. I didn't know exactly what this vision meant at the time.

Before finding a place to live, before heading to see my university, I went straight to visit him. I just had to go see Jack. There he was at the train station, a huge goofy smile on his face, and an even bigger goofy smile wrapped on mine when I realised I'd returned *home*. We didn't waste any time *this time*.

We wove easily back into each other's lives and hearts. We moved into a sand-kissed beach shack. We fell in love hard. He said, 'I want you to write *whatever you want to write*.' My heart sighed a shuddering relief that pulsed magic through my veins.

Two years later I graduated with sweat-driven HDs for my manuscript. We went to Bali to celebrate. I wrote WRITER on the customs slip on the plane home. I scored a job for a leading Australian lifestyle magazine company that very day. I was an editor within months.

And the rest is history. And I *don't care* that it's a cliche. That's me, baby. A big fuckin' sunshiney ol' cliché.

Miracles are possible

When I met Jack halfway through my trip through Latin America, I was bloody tired. I'd seen sloths and sniffed cocaine and swum with sea lions in the Galapagos. I'd exhausted myriad character roles on my quest to find myself. I had no energy left for games or romance and so we sat, just me and Jack, as friends. We talked. We ate, drank and hiked. We endured sickness and storms all the way to the top of Machu Picchu. I told him everything about me, the good and the bad.

When we are our authentic selves, miracles happen. I don't need to explain the rest – as a thoughtful and intelligent writer and reader, you can see the meaning in the gaps.

You don't really know ... but you do it anyway

People told me many limiting beliefs on my journey like, 'Writers don't make money' and 'You won't find happiness elsewhere. You have to be happy with what you have.' But in 2015, I got on the plane anyway. Maybe they were right, or maybe they weren't. All I knew was, I had to follow my heart. I cried, then smiled, and cried all the way to Mexico. I didn't know if I was ever returning. And then I saw things and met new people that shook up my life and taught me that what I was searching for was possible.

Your story may not be about a flight to the other side of the world. Your story might be about going skydiving, writing that book, enrolling in that degree, joining that new dating app, telling your parents about your true sexual preference. But if it's coming from your heart, you must listen. (Although I highly recommend travel for shaking up your life fast and opening your perspectives!)

What if you did it? And what if magic happened?

What I was actually looking for was a deep and unwavering love of my *Self*, my spirit, my callings. I had to wander a long time, but I never knew what I was looking for until I learned how to love myself for exactly who I was. And it all started with listening to the callings of my heart, wandering the world, and putting pen to paper.

When we invest time and energy into ourselves, we grow – and our capacity to inspire positive change in the world grows. When we empower our lives with creativity, our heart coherence expands into the positive, our brainwaves optimise, our vibration changes, and spirit enters the room. And that's how our whole reality shifts.

When we empower our lives with creativity, our heart coherence expands into the positive, our brainwaves optimise, our vibration changes, and spirit enters the room. And that's how our whole reality shifts.

The only way to learn to become the writer I'd always known I was destined to become was to open my heart and my mind. And that meant learning, taking risks, facing fear, and understanding it's OK, in fact it's necessary, to fail. And then get up, girl, *just get up*, and keep writing – and one day find a way to publish my work.

To get this book published, it wasn't as hard as I thought it would be, in the end. A short story of mine was published by *The Kind Press,* which led to an editing gig – which led to writing workshops offered to their author programs – which led to a unique deal and a brilliant collaboration which has now opened up accessible publishing opportunities for my *HeartWriting* clients. I have now found myself a trustworthy and aligned publisher to work with on multiple future projects. But all this happened because I didn't rush. I waited until spirit showed me the best way for me. *Slow and steady wins the race.* My eternal thanks to Natasha Gilmour and *The Kind Press* for so lovingly taking me on – and publishing this book so beautifully.

I'd like to thank Jack: my best friend, travel buddy and life partner, for letting me write about you so constantly and openly, for enthusiastically supporting my dream – and for being the guy who told me to 'write whatever you want to write'. I also want to thank my family. Perhaps it took a lot in the beginning to believe that a creative writer could make it – but I did, and it warms my heart that you all are so crazy-proud of this whacky little dreamer! Thank you in particular to Mum, for saying to me several years ago, 'no matter who comes out of the woodwork, or what anyone says – don't let them stop you from writing your words. You have a gift, and your words are needed.' It felt like the words were coming directly from your heart.

Thank you to Debra Adelaide and Delia Falconer, my creative writing lecturers (two remarkably gifted and accomplished Australian authors) who believed in my unique work from the start (including my high-octane travel stories and experimental memoir!). You are the mentors who modelled and shaped every outrageous possibility in writing for me – while keeping me focused and grounded. The university classroom isn't the same as *HeartWriting*, but you both taught your gifts with the heart I needed.

My deepest thanks to Monica McKenzie, Dharawal-Yuin woman, Deputy Chair of the Aboriginal Advisory Panel for Central Coast Council, and lecturer from the University of Newcastle. You generously offered me your time and wisdom in explaining to me your family's understanding of the Dreaming. Your personal connection to Country and its stories, and your connection to me (as a recent *HeartWriting* student) was invaluable in helping me explain the nuances of cultural storytelling with respect and grace.

Thank you to David Naylor, renowned and retired Australian journalist, editor, and publisher. I was so lucky to meet you during our master's and I'm beyond grateful that you took me under your wing. Without your knowledge, friendship, and mentorship, I'm not sure I would have come so far. Connection is indeed everything. Constructive feedback over a couple of beers before the train home is *life* for a budding writer. At the time, I had no idea I'd become not only a published author but also an editor. You taught me how to kindly bring out the best in a writer – starting with myself.

And thank you to my golden girlfriends – you know who you are! – my fellow writers and friends who never fail to help me unravel a long rambling thread of thought, or provide just the right word when I've lost all vocabulary. What a gift it is to have friends who live from the heart, who challenge each other to honour our highest potential – without skipping the belly laughs or skimping on the wine. I always leave our 'meetings' with ten new ideas and a full heart. Now *that's* a creative community.

Which leads me beautifully to a heartfelt thank you to the hundreds of dedicated *HeartWriting* students who have become not only my greatest source of inspiration, but my closest friends. I've never had so many brilliant, soulful creatives in my life, all because I followed my heart.

Lastly, a huge thank you to Kim White from Safety Bay Yoga Centre in Western Australia, for being the first (and best) yoga teacher all those years ago. You gently and beautifully guided me through my first awakening, followed by many years of your divine classes that inevitably shaped my style as a yoga teacher. And thank you to your beautiful wife, Sylvia, for being my spiritual mentor and the feminine goddess I aspired to become. You lit the path for me. You taught me about food, art, life, love, and theta healing. And you trusted I would find my way. The universe indeed conspired to bring both of you into my life during those shaky years. The books you lent me, the words whispered to me, and the philosophy you both taught me – have resulted in this book, and my new life. I hope everyone finds themselves a Kim and Sylvia: unconditional light and love. *Thank you, thank you, thank you.*

Many thanks for reading this book – from the bottom of my heart! – and many blessings to you on your *HeartWriting* journey. I am beyond grateful that you landed on these pages. Somehow, we will always be connected – do you feel that too? Hopefully these words have been as healing for you as they have been healing for me to write and share them.

With all my love,

Just start by placing a hand on your heart: and listen to the author within.

Learn the magic of *HeartWriting*® with Rose Mascaro – Australian author, editor, and creative writing specialist, who is passionate about teaching writers how to connect with their most authentic, heart-led words.

From facing fears, slowing down from a high-speed life, connecting with your heart and savouring the craft of words, you'll be taken on a meaningful journey that will transform you into a world-class, *heart-led* writer.

You'll also explore the science and spirituality of the heart, the evolution and theory of narrative, and why storytelling remains at the heart of human connection.

When you set your authentic words free they have the power to become a healing balm for the world.

Recommended Reading

Aristotle. (1996). *Poetics* (M. Heath, Trans.). Penguin.
Brach, T. (2003). *Radical acceptance: Embracing your life with the heart of a Buddha*. Bantam Books.
Cameron, J. (1992). *The artist's way: A spiritual path to higher creativity*. TarcherPerigee.
Campbell, J., Cousineau, P., & Brown, S. L. (2003). *The hero's journey: Joseph Campbell on his life and work*. New World Library.
Clear, J. (2018). *Atomic habits: An easy & proven way to build good habits & break bad ones*. Penguin.
Coelho, P. (1993). *The alchemist* (A. R. Clarke, Trans.). HarperTorch. (Originally published 1988)
Courtille, B. (2025). *Buddhism for yogis*. Courtille.
Csikszentmihalyi, M. (1990). *Flow: The psychology of optimal experience*. Harper & Row.
Dass, R. (1971). *Be here now*. Lama Foundation.
Evaristo, B. (2019). *Girl, woman, other*. Hamish Hamilton.
Freytag, G. (1896). *Freytag's technique of the drama: An exposition of dramatic composition and art* (E. J. MacEwan, Trans.). Scott, Foresman & Co. (Originally published in German in 1863)
Gilbert, E. (2006). *Eat, pray, love: One woman's search for everything across Italy, India, and Indonesia*. Viking.
Gladwell, M. (2008). *Outliers: The story of success*. Little, Brown.
Iyengar, B. K. S. (1966). *Light on yoga*. George Allen & Unwin.
Iyengar, B. K. S. (2008). *Yoga: The path to holistic health* (Rev. ed.). DK Publishing.
Jeffers, S. (1987). *Feel the fear and do it anyway*. Ballantine Books.
Jung, C. G. (2012). *The red book: A reader's edition*. W. W. Norton.
Kabat-Zinn, J. (1994). *Wherever you go, there you are: Mindfulness meditation in everyday life*. Hyperion.
Kahlert, S. (2019). *Advaita Vedanta for ordinary people*. Inspiring Publishers.

Murakami, H. (2022). *Novelist as a vocation*. Harvill Secker.
Ruiz, D. J. (2023). *The shaman's path to freedom*. Hierophant Publishing.
Satchidananda, S. S. (2012). *The Yoga Sutras of Patanjali: Translation and commentary by Sri Swami Satchidananda*. Integral Yoga Publications.
Smith, D., Schlaepfer, P., Major, K., et al. (2017). Cooperation and the evolution of hunter-gatherer storytelling. Nature Communications, 8, 1853. https://doi.org/10.1038/s41467-017-02036-8
Winton, T. (1991). *Cloudstreet*. McPhee Gribble.
Woolf, V. (2001). *A room of one's own*. Penguin Books. (Originally published 1929)
Yunkaporta, T. (2023). *Right story, wrong story: Adventures in Indigenous thinking*. Text Publishing Company.
Zaki, J. (2021, August). *How to escape the cynicism trap* [Video]. TED Conferences. Retrieved from https://www.ted.com/talks/jamil_zaki_how_to_escape_the_cynicism_trap

Endnotes

1. Grayling, A. C. (2024, September 17). *The meaning of life in a technological age* [Audio podcast episode]. Sydney Writers' Festival. Retrieved from https://www.swf.org.au/stories/2024/podcast-ac-grayling-the-meaning-of-life-in-a-technological-age
2. King, S. (2000). *On writing: A memoir of the craft* (pp. 91–92). Scribner.
3. D. Childre, H. Martin, D. Rozman, & R. McCraty. (2016). *Heart intelligence: Connecting with the intuitive guidance of the heart.* Waterfront Digital Press.
4. Roy, A. (2004). *The God of small things* (p. 308). Random House.
5. Saunders, G. (2017). *Lincoln in the bardo* (p.101). Random House.
6. Fitzgerald, F. S. (2004). *The great Gatsby* (p. 39). Scribner. (Originally published 1925).

www.ingramcontent.com/pod-product-compliance
Lightning Source LLC
Chambersburg PA
CBHW020526080526
44583CB00013B/749